The Yummy

GREEN MOUNTAIN

WOOD PELLET GRILL

COOKBOOK

OVER 200 TASTY IDEAS THAT WILL AMAZE YOUR NEIGHBORS AND DELICIOUS SAUCES CLASSICAL AND CONTEMPORARY RECIPES

REBECCA KIRBY

CONTENTS

INTRODUCTION

How the Green Mountain Wood Pellet Grill Works

While there are still things that you must do manually as you use a pellet grill, and it is important to pay attention to them, these grills do much of the difficult work for you, like maintaining the desired temperature.

The first thing you must do is fill the hopper with wood pellets. The amount of pellets you will need depends on what kind of cooking you are doing and what temperature will have to be maintained. The manual that comes with the grill should have a guide for this.

Once the grill transfers the wood pellets to the firepot and ignites, you can set the temperature you need with a dial. Lower settings take longer to cook the food, but they also keep the meat moist. This dial will send the information to the auger, the part that transfers pellets.

So long as you put the proper amount of pellets in at the start, the grill will continue cooking for as long as it needs to. Some newer models even have an alert feature that will notify you if the amount of wood pellets gets too low.

The Benefits of Your Green Mountain Wood Pellet Grill

1.   The Flavor

This is where you have to start this discussion. Yes, there are other benefits you can read about below, but the real benefit of owning a pellet grill is the quality and flavor of the food you can make on them. The reason professional barbecue chefs use wood is because it provides the best flavor. And unlike gas or charcoal, you can vary the flavor with the type of wood pellets you choose, and you can even mix and match to create the perfect flavor for whatever you put on your grill. Our handy find your flavor guide below is great for a quick reference, or you can check out our more detailed guide on selecting the right flavor of pellets.

2.   The Ease of Use

Many people get a little intimidated at the thought of using a pellet grill, but those fears are unfounded. Though a pellet grill is different from the standard gas and charcoal grills many people are used to, they're surprisingly user friendly. Green Mountain wood pellet grill have controls that you can simply set and forget. Green Mountain wood pellet grill offer a number of features that make grilling shockingly easy.

> One button start up – no lighter fluid needed.
> Regardless of the temperature or weather outside, the Grilla and Silverbac keep the temperature within a ten degree range of your set temperature, letting you cook like a pro with zero effort!
> Our pellet grills never have flare ups, so you don't need to worry about your eyebrows.
> You won't oversmoke your food.

With a pellet grill, it's really that easy. You want a perfectly slow smoked brisket? You might be surprised to learn that this doesn't require you to spend 14 hours of your time and attention anymore. With a pellet grill there's no learning curve for making great food. It's literally as easy as filling up the hopper with your preferred flavor of pellets, pushing a button and tossing your meat on the grill. The grill will control the temperature and all you need to do is remove it from the grill when it's done. It can't get any easier than that, can it?

3. The Versatility

Your old gas grill just can't hang with a pellet grill when it comes to the variety of ways you can cook with it. With precise control of cooking temperatures between 180 degrees to 500 degrees you can sear, smoke, roast, and bake with a pellet grill. Why buy a smoker and a grill when you can have both in one well-constructed package? Check out our recipes section to see the incredible range of food you can produce on a pellet grill, everything from brisket, steaks and burgers to shrimp bruschetta and even pecan pie.

Useful Tricks for Using Your Green Mountain Wood Pellet Grill

1. USE THE UPPER RACKS OF YOUR Green Mountain WOOD PELLET GRILL

Upper racks are great accessories for pellet grills. Not only do they increase the cooking capacity per once grilling session, but upper racks can also decrease the radiant heat releasing from the grease tray.

The meat from the upper racks receives lighter heat, so it is appropriate to cook tender pieces. And the thicker chunk of food can be cooked on the lower rack.

Besides, you can put a water pan under that rack to maintain the ideal temperature for a long brisket cook.

2. USE YOUR Green Mountain WOOD PELLET GRILL LIKE YOU USE YOUR OVEN

One of the most straightforward tips to create tastier dishes is to use the pellet grill the same way as using the oven.

Not every food works well with smoke, but how can you know if you haven't tried once, right? Just be brave and creative when mixing the menu, and you can be surprised then.

Any recipe for roasting and baking in your oven can be applied to the smoker. By keeping the same cooking time or alternating cooking period, you can compare how food quality varies between the two devices.

For instance, baking a cake in an oven is too familiar, so why not try grilling in the pellet smoker instead? Making a cake in the oven takes 30 minutes, but you can alternate to 45 minutes or an hour for a grill. The result might come out as not as good as you expect, but, how can you learn if you don't try, right?

3. USE THE REVERSE SEARING

Experienced chefs recommend reverse searing because it can ensure cooked food. Let's go through the process and learn how to do it. Please notice that this method works better on beef slices that are 4 to 5 cm thick.

Firstly, take the meat out from the freezer and wait until it defrosts completely. Then, put the meat on water-absorbing cooking paper to suck water from the meat. Later, warm up the grill at 446 Fahrenheit degree (230 Celsius degree).

The second step is to add salt, sauce, etc. into the food. Wait about 20 minutes for the meat can absorb the mixture better.

Next, put the meat into the pellet smoker for 6 to 8 minutes to reach the medium-rare state (130 Fahrenheit degree/ 54.4 Celsius degree). Then, take out the food and wait for about 5 to 7 minutes.

Finally, half-frying the meat in total 90 seconds with 45 minutes on each side. You should not press the food because juice extraction can decrease the taste of the dish.

4. KEEP TRACK OF THE TEMPERATURE BY USING A THERMOMETER

We are unable to keep track of the inside environment of the smoker just by the sighting. We suggest you use a thermometer to check the heat periodically.

Most people use a clock to set the cooking time so that once it rings, you know whether the dish is ready to serve. However, this is just a presumption based on experience, so there can be risks of overcooking or unripe dishes. So, why don't you choose the safer options instead? A thermometer can solve all these problems.

Besides, there are some grilling experts saying that once you open the grill door, you can't cook anymore. That's true! The heat can escape to the outside environment, and the cooking process will be affected.

Hence, it's better to purchase a smoker with an integrated thermometer for a better grilling experience. Also, the integrated thermometer will help you to check the temperature without opening the grill's door.

Significant Tips for Cleaning Your Green Mountain Wood Pellet Grill

1. Invest in a Grill Cover.

If a Traeger is stored outside during wet weather, water can get into the Pellet Hopper. When pellets get wet, they expand and can clog the auger. Additionally, a pellet grill cannot cook with wet wood. If you do not have a cover, take extra care to keep the pellet hopper covered and away from any water.

2. Clean your Grease Drain Pan.

Changing the aluminum foil on the grease pan often is a great first step, but to get the most out of your pellet grill you must clean underneath the foil as well. Use a metal spatula to scrape the extra grease and debris from the grease pan and the grease drain tube. Grease is easiest to clean when it is slightly warm. If the grease drain tube becomes plugged or blocked, a grease fire can result. Clean those areas periodically to prevent build-up.

3. Empty your Grease Bucket.

This job is not pretty, but it is pretty easy. Empty your grease into something you can discard, such as a plastic cup. Do not pour grease down the sink drain or into the gutter. Be sure to let the grease cool thoroughly before discarding it. Rinse your bucket with hot, soapy water to remove any remaining grease. To make future clean up easier, line your grease bucket with aluminum foil.

4. Wipe Down your Grill Exterior.

To keep that powder coating looking like new, use warm soapy water to cut through any grease. Do not use oven cleaners, abrasive cleaners, or scouring pads on the outside of your grill.

5. Remove extra ash from the Firepot.

Periodically remove the Porcelain Grill Grate, Grease Drain Pan, and Heat Baffle to clean the ash in and around the Firepot. This step can be fast and easy by using a standard shop vac. Make sure all grill components are cold before vacuuming up the extra ash. We recommend cleaning your grill once for every 5 times you use it. These tips will help keep your grill running beautifully for years to come!

SEAFOOD RECIPES

Smoked Crab Legs

Servings: 4
Cooking Time: 30 Minutes

Ingredients:
- 4 Whole crab legs
- 4 Tablespoon butter, melted
- 1/2 Cup Texas Spicy BBQ Sauce
- salt and pepper
- 1 Tablespoon Fin & Feather Rub

Directions:
1. Supply your smoker with wood pellets and follow the start-up procedure. Preheat the grill, with the lid closed, to 250° F.
2. Place the crab legs directly on the grill grate and smoke for 20 minutes. Grill: 250 °F
3. While the crab is smoking, make the sauce. In a medium bowl, combine melted butter, Traeger Texas Spicy BBQ sauce, salt, pepper and Traeger Fin & Feather Rub.
4. After 20 minutes of cooking, brush the crab legs with the BBQ sauce mixture. Continue to cook for another 10 minutes reserving the remaining sauce to serve. Remove crab legs from the grill, and serve with melted butter and BBQ sauce mixture. Enjoy!

Cajun-blackened Shrimp

Servings: 4
Cooking Time: 20 Minutes

Ingredients:
- 1 pound peeled and deveined shrimp, with tails on
- 1 batch Cajun Rub

- 8 tablespoons (1 stick) butter
- ¼ cup Worcestershire sauce

Directions:
1. Supply your smoker with wood pellets and follow the start-up procedure. Preheat the grill, with the lid closed, to 450°F and place a cast-iron skillet on the grill grate. Wait about 10 minutes after your grill has reached temperature, allowing the skillet to get hot.
2. Meanwhile, season the shrimp all over with the rub.
3. When the skillet is hot, place the butter in it to melt. Once the butter melts, stir in the Worcestershire sauce.
4. Add the shrimp and gently stir to coat. Smoke-braise the shrimp for about 10 minutes per side, until opaque and cooked through. Remove the shrimp from the grill and serve immediately.

Garlic Blackened Catfish

Servings: 4
Cooking Time: 10 Minutes

Ingredients:
- ½ Cup Cajun Seasoning
- ¼ Tsp Cayenne Pepper
- 1 Tsp Granulated Garlic
- 1 Tsp Ground Thyme
- 1 Tsp Onion Powder
- 1 Tsp Ground Oregano
- 1 Tsp Pepper
- 4 (5-Oz.) Skinless Catfish Fillets
- 1 Tbsp Smoked Paprika
- 1 Stick Unsalted Butter

Directions:

1. In a small bowl, combine the Cajun seasoning, smoked paprika, onion powder, granulated garlic, ground oregano, ground thyme, pepper and cayenne pepper.

2. Sprinkle fish with salt and let rest for 20 minutes.

3. Supply your smoker with wood pellets and follow the start-up procedure. Preheat the grill, with the lid closed, to 450° F. If you're using a gas or charcoal grill, set it up for medium-high heat. Place cast iron skillet on the grill and let it preheat.

4. While grill is preheating, sprinkle catfish fillets with seasoning mixture, pressing gently to adhere. Add half the butter to preheated cast iron skillet and swirl to coat, add more butter if needed. Place fillets in hot skillet and cook 3-5 minutes or until a dark crust has been formed. Flip and cook an additional 3-5 minutes or until the fish flakes apart when pressed gently with your finger.

5. Remove fish from grill and sprinkle evenly with fresh parsley. Serve with lemon wedges and enjoy!

Grilled Garlic Shrimp With Cajun Dip

Servings: 4
Cooking Time: 15 Minutes

Ingredients:
- 1 Grated Garlic Cloves, Peeled
- 1 Tsp Lemon Juice
- ½ Cup Mayonnaise
- 2 Tbsp Olive Oil
- 1 ½ Tbsp Hickory Bacon Rub
- Scallions
- ½ Lb Shelled And Deveined Shrimp
- 1 Cup Sour Cream

Directions:
1. Supply your smoker with wood pellets and follow the start-up procedure. Preheat the grill, with the lid closed, to 350° F. If you're using a gas or charcoal grill, set it to medium heat.

2. In a glass mixing bowl, add mayonnaise, sour cream, Cajun seasoning, garlic, lemon juice, hot sauce, and Hickory Bacon. Whisk together until well combined.

3. Cajun shrimp: In a small bowl, add shrimp, olive oil, Cajun-style seasoning and Hickory Bacon seasoning and toss to combine. Set aside.

4. Transfer dip mixture into cast iron ramekin or small Dutch oven and cover with foil. Place on preheated grill and cook for 10-15 minutes, or until dip begins to bubble along the edges. At the same time, place cast iron pan on grill and add shrimp. Cook for about 3-5 minutes on each side or until shrimp are opaque.

5. Remove dip from grill and top with Cajun shrimp and scallions. Serve warm alongside garlic toast squares and enjoy!

Cold-smoked Salmon Gravlax

Servings: 6
Cooking Time: 30 Minutes

Ingredients:
- 1 Cup kosher salt
- 1 Cup sugar
- 1 Tablespoon freshly ground black pepper
- 2 Pound Sushi-Grad Salmon Fillet, Skin-on, Pin Bones Removed
- 2 Bunch Dill Weed, fresh
- capers, drained
- red onion, sliced
- cream cheese

- lemons

Directions:

1. In a bowl stir together the salt, sugar and black pepper until thoroughly combined. On a work surface, turn salmon skin side up and sprinkle about half of salt mixture all over and rub in.

2. Arrange half the dill on the bottom of a baking dish large enough to hold the salmon. Set salmon skin side down on bed of dill.

3. Rub remaining salt mixture all over top and sides of salmon, then top with remaining dill. Cover with plastic, then top with a weight on a smaller baking dish or a plate with cans of beans on top, then place in refrigerator and allow to cure for 2 days.

4. Remove salmon from refrigerator, rinse under cold water and pat dry with paper towels. Allow to sit at room temperature on the counter for 1 hour

5. Supply your smoker with wood pellets and follow the start-up procedure. Preheat the grill, with the lid closed, to 180° F. Place salmon onto a baking pan. Fill another baking pan with ice and place baking pan with salmon over ice. Place onto grill and smoke for 30 minutes.

6. Remove from grill and slice thin. Serve with capers, red onion, dill, cream cheese, and lemon. Enjoy!

Grilled Whole Steelhead Fillet

Servings: 6
Cooking Time: 30 Minutes

Ingredients:

- (2-1/2 to 3 lb) steelhead or salmon fillet, skin-on
- 2 Tablespoon Montana Mex Sweet Seasoning

- 1 Teaspoon Montana Mex Jalapeño Seasoning Blend
- 1 Teaspoon Montana Mex Mild Chile Seasoning Blend
- 2 Tablespoon Montana Mex Avocado Oil
- 2 Tablespoon freshly grated ginger
- 1 lemon, thinly sliced

Directions:

1. Coat fillet evenly with all three dry seasonings, avocado oil, grated ginger and thinly sliced lemon.

2. Supply your smoker with wood pellets and follow the start-up procedure. Preheat the grill, with the lid closed, to 380° F.

3. Place the fish skin-side down on the grill grate and cook for 20 minutes. Grill: 380 °F

4. Remove fillet from grill and let rest for 5 minutes. Enjoy!

Alder Smoked Scallops With Citrus & Garlic Butter Sauce

Servings: 4
Cooking Time: 35 Minutes

Ingredients:

- 2 Pound large dry sea scallops
- kosher salt
- freshly ground black pepper
- 8 Tablespoon salted butter, melted
- 1 Clove garlic, minced
- 1 Small orange
- 1/4 Teaspoon Worcestershire sauce
- 1 1/2 Teaspoon fresh chopped parsley or tarragon
- flat-leaf parsley, for serving

Directions:

1. Wash the scallops under cold running water and thoroughly pat dry on paper towels. Remove

any tags of abductor muscle tissue you find on the sides of the scallops.

2. Arrange the scallops on a baking sheet fitted with a cooling rack, and season with salt and pepper.

3. Supply your smoker with wood pellets and follow the start-up procedure. Preheat the grill, with the lid closed, to 165° F.

4. Place the baking sheet with the scallops on the grill grate and smoke for 20 minutes.

5. While your scallops are smoking, make your sauce. Melt the butter in a small saucepan over medium-low heat. Add a pinch of salt, garlic, Worcestershire sauce, zest and juice from half of the orange, and parsley. Simmer for 5 minutes. Keep warm.

6. Remove the baking sheet with the scallops from the grill and set aside. Increase the temperature to 400°F and preheat, lid closed. Optional: Place an oyster bed or oyster pan in the grill to preheat. These heavy iron pans are a great way to sear the scallops. Grill: 400 °F

7. Return the baking sheet with the scallops to the grill, brush with the butter sauce, reserving some for serving. Roast until just opaque and tender, 10 to 15 minutes. The time will depend on how thick the scallops are. Do not overcook. If you are using an oyster pan, brush each compartment lightly with olive oil to prevent sticking. Spoon butter sauce on each of the scallops, reserving some for serving.

8. Serve the scallops hot with a little more orange zest, fresh parsley and the the warm citrus and garlic butter sauce. Enjoy!

Florentine Shrimp Al Cartoccio

Servings: 4

Cooking Time: 13 Minutes

Ingredients:
- 6 tbsp unsalted butter, melted
- ½ cup heavy whipping cream
- ½ cup grated Parmesan cheese
- 2 garlic cloves, peeled and minced
- 1 cup thinly sliced button mushrooms, cleaned and destemmed
- 1 cup baby spinach leaves
- 2 tbsp chopped sun-dried, oil-packed tomatoes
- ½ tsp dried oregano
- ½ tsp dried basil
- ½ tsp crushed red pepper flakes, plus more
- ½ tsp coarse salt
- ½ tsp freshly ground black pepper
- 20 to 24 jumbo shrimp, about 1lb (450g) total, peeled and deveined
- sprigs of fresh rosemary, basil, thyme, or oregano

Directions:

1. Supply your smoker with wood pellets and follow the start-up procedure. Preheat the grill, with the lid closed, to 400° F.

2. In a large bowl, combine the butter and whipping cream. Stir in the Parmesan, garlic, mushrooms, spinach, tomatoes, oregano, basil, red pepper flakes, and salt and pepper. Add the shrimp and stir gently to coat.

3. Place four 12-inch (30.5cm) sheets of wide heavy-duty aluminum foil on a workspace and pull up the sides. Divide the shrimp mixture evenly between the sheets of foil. Roll and crimp the top and sides of the foil to create sealed packages.

4. Place the packets seam side up on the grate and grill until the shrimp are cooked through,

about 10 to 13 minutes. (You can carefully open one package to check on the shrimp.)

5. Transfer the packets to plates. Carefully open the packets to avoid any steam. Scatter fresh herbs over the shrimp before serving.

Baked Whole Fish In Sea Salt

Servings: 4

Cooking Time: 30 Minutes

Ingredients:
- 3 Pound Whole Branzino, (1.5 each)
- 10 Sprig thyme sprigs
- 1 Medium lemon, thinly sliced
- 5 Cup sea salt
- 10 Whole egg white
- olive oil
- 1 Whole lemon juice

Directions:

1. Supply your smoker with wood pellets and follow the start-up procedure. Preheat the grill, with the lid closed, to High heat.

2. Clip the fins and remove the gills from the fish. Stuff cavity with thyme and lemon slices. Whip the egg whites to soft peaks and fold in the sea salt.

3. Place directly on the grill grate and bake for 30 minutes or until a thermometer poked through the salt crust and into the flesh of the fish registers an internal temperature of 135-140 degrees F. Remove fish from the grill and let stand 10 minutes.

4. Using a wooden spoon, strike the crust to crack it open and brush remaining salt from the surface of the fish.

5. Remove the skin and drizzle fish with good olive oil and a squeeze of lemon. Enjoy!

Grilled Artichoke Cheese Salmon

Servings: 12

Cooking Time: 270 Minutes

Ingredients:
- 28 Oz Artichoke Hearts, Whole, Canned
- 1/2 Cup Breadcrumbs
- 1/2 Cup Brown Sugar
- 8 Oz Cream Cheese
- 1 Tbsp Garlic Powder
- 1 Cup Italian Cheese Blend, Shredded
- 1/4 Cup Kosher Salt
- 1 Cup Mayonnaise
- 2 Tsp Olive Oil
- 1 Tbsp Onion Powder
- 1/2 Cup Parmesan Cheese
- 2 Tbsp Parsley, Chopped
- Blackened Sriracha Rub
- 1 1/4 Lbs Salmon, Fillet, Scaled And Deboned
- Sour Cream
- 1/2 Tsp White Pepper, Ground

Directions:

1. In a small mixing bowl, whisk together the brown sugar, salt, garlic powder, onion powder, and white pepper. This will make twice the cure needed, so be sure and place the remaining half in a resealable plastic bag and save for smoking fish at a later date.

2. Lay a sheet of plastic wrap on a sheet tray and sprinkle a thin layer of the cure on it. Place the salmon skin-side down on top of the cure, then sprinkle a couple tablespoons of cure on top. Gently press the cure on top of the salmon flesh, then wrap in plastic wrap.

3. Refrigerate for 8 hours, or overnight.

4. Remove salmon from the refrigerator and wash off the cure in the sink, under cold water.

5. Blot salmon with a paper towel, then set salmon skin side on a wire rack. Dry at room temperature for two hours, or until a yellowish shimmer appears on the salmon.

6. Supply your smoker with wood pellets and follow the start-up procedure. Preheat the grill, with the lid closed, to 250° F. If using a gas, charcoal or other grill, set it to low, indirect heat.

7. Place the salmon in the upper cabinet. Smoke for 2 hours, then increase the grill temperature to 350° F to maintain a cabinet temperature of 225°F and smoke another 1 to 2 hours, until salmon reaches an internal temperature of 145° F.

8. Remove salmon from the cabinet and set aside to rest for 15 minutes, then flake apart. Reserve ½ cup to top dip after grilling.

9. While the salmon is resting, drain the artichokes, then skewer onto metal skewers (if using wooden skewers, make sure to soak in water for 1 hour prior to grilling, or you can use a grill basket as well).

10. Season with Blackened Sriracha, then set on the grill. Grill for 2 to 3 minutes, until lightly browned.

11. Remove from the grill, cool slightly, then roughly chop. Set aside.

12. In a mixing bowl, combine shredded Italian cheese, grated parmesan, breadcrumbs and parsley. Set aside.

13. Place cream cheese, mayonnaise, and sour cream in a cast iron skillet. Stir frequently, with a wooden spoon, for about 5 minutes, until the mixture is smooth.

14. Carefully fold in flaked salmon and grilled artichoke hearts, then spread breadcrumb mixture over dip.

15. Drizzle with olive oil, then close the grill lid and bake for 25 to 30 minutes, until dip begins to bubble around the edges, and cheese begins to caramelize on top.

16. Remove dip from the grill, top with reserved salmon and a pinch of parsley. Serve warm with bagel chips, crackers, or crusty bread.

Lobster Tail

Servings: 2
Cooking Time: 25 Minutes

Ingredients:
- 2 lobster tails
- Salt
- Freshly ground black pepper
- 1 batch Lemon Butter Mop for Seafood

Directions:
1. Supply your smoker with wood pellets and follow the start-up procedure. Preheat the grill, with the lid closed, to 375°F.

2. Using kitchen shears, slit the top of the lobster shells, through the center, nearly to the tail. Once cut, expose as much meat as you can through the cut shell.

3. Season the lobster tails all over with salt and pepper.

4. Place the tails directly on the grill grate and grill until their internal temperature reaches 145°F. Remove the lobster from the grill and serve with the mop on the side for dipping.

Seared Bluefin Tuna Steaks

Servings: 2
Cooking Time: 5 Minutes

Ingredients:
- 3 Whole Tuna, steak
- olive oil

- salt and pepper
- soy sauce
- Sriracha

Directions:

1. Lightly baste both sides of tuna steaks in olive oil; sprinkle sea salt and ground pepper on each side.

2. Supply your smoker with wood pellets and follow the start-up procedure. Preheat the grill, with the lid closed, to High heat.

3. Grill tuna steaks on each side for 2 to 2-1/2 minutes.

4. Remove tuna from grill and allow to cool slightly.

5. Cut into 1/2 - 3/4" pieces. Serve with a mixture of Soy Sauce and Sriracha. Enjoy!"

Lemon Lobster Rolls

Servings: 4
Cooking Time: 35 Minutes

Ingredients:

- 1/2 Cup Butter
- 4 Hot Dog Bun(S)
- 1 Lemon, Whole
- 4 Lobster, Tail
- 1/4 Cup Mayo
- Pepper

Directions:

1. Supply your smoker with wood pellets and follow the start-up procedure. Preheat the grill, with the lid closed, to 300° F.

2. Using kitchen shears, cut the shell of the tail and crack in half so that the meat is exposed. Pour in butter and season with pepper. Place the tails meat side up on the grill and cook until the shell has turned red and the meat is white, about 35 minutes.

3. Remove from the grill and separate the shell from the meat. Place the meat in a bowl with mayo, lemon juice and rind and season with pepper. Stir to combine and evenly distribute into the hot dog buns.

Bacon Wrapped Scallops

Servings: 8
Cooking Time: 20 Minutes

Ingredients:

- 24 jumbo deep sea diver scallops, dry-packed
- 1/2 Cup butter
- salt
- freshly ground black pepper
- 1 Clove garlic, minced
- 12 Slices thin-cut bacon, cut in half crosswise
- lemon wedges, for serving

Directions:

1. Remove the small, crescent-shaped muscle from the side of each scallop, if still attached. Dry the scallops thoroughly on paper towels, then transfer to a medium bowl.

2. Melt butter in a small saucepan, add garlic and cook for 1 minute. Let cool slightly then pour over the scallops. Season with salt and pepper and gently toss to coat.

3. Wrap a piece of bacon around each scallop and secure with a toothpick.

4. Supply your smoker with wood pellets and follow the start-up procedure. Preheat the grill, with the lid closed, to 400° F.

5. Arrange the scallops directly on the grill grate. Grill for 15 to 20 minutes, or until the scallop is opaque and the bacon has begun to crisp. If desired, you can turn the scallops on their side, bacon-side down, turning occasionally to crisp the bacon. Do not overcook. Grill: 400 °F

6. Transfer the scallops to a platter and serve with lemon wedges.

Mexican Mahi Mahi With Baja Cabbage Slaw

Servings: 4
Cooking Time: 10 Minutes

Ingredients:

- 1½lb (680g) skinless mahi mahi, cod, or other firm white fish fillets
- coarse salt
- freshly ground black pepper
- chili powder
- lime wedges
- for the slaw
- 2 cups finely shredded green cabbage
- 2 cups finely shredded purple cabbage
- 4 tbsp reduced-fat mayo
- 2 tsp hot sauce, plus more
- 2 tsp freshly squeezed lime juice
- ½ tsp coarse salt
- for the marinade
- ¼ cup freshly squeezed orange juice
- ¼ cup freshly squeezed lime juice
- 2 tbsp extra virgin olive oil

Directions:

1. In a medium bowl, make the slaw by combining the ingredients. Stir well. Transfer to a serving bowl. Cover and refrigerate until ready to serve.

2. Place the fish fillets in a baking dish and pour the orange and lime juices and olive oil over them. Turn the fillets to coat thoroughly. Cover and refrigerate for 15 to 20 minutes.

3. Supply your smoker with wood pellets and follow the start-up procedure. Preheat the grill, with the lid closed, to 450° F.

4. Drain the fish and pat dry with paper towels. (Discard the marinade.) Season the fillets on both sides with salt and pepper and chili powder. Place the fillets on the grate and grill until golden brown, about 4 to 5 minutes per side, turning with a thin-bladed spatula.

5. Transfer the fish to a platter. Serve with the slaw and lime wedges.

Moules Marinières With Garlic Butter Sauce

Servings: 4
Cooking Time: 12 Minutes

Ingredients:

- 3lb (1.4kg) fresh mussels, scrubbed under cold running water and debearded
- lemon wedges
- crusty bread (optional)
- for the sauce
- 6 tbsp unsalted butter
- 3 garlic cloves, peeled and minced
- 1 cup dry white wine or hard cider
- 1 tbsp freshly squeezed lemon juice
- 2 tsp hot sauce, plus more
- coarse salt
- freshly ground black pepper
- 2 tbsp chopped fresh curly parsley or tarragon

Directions:

1. Supply your smoker with wood pellets and follow the start-up procedure. Preheat the grill, with the lid closed, to 450° F.

2. In a small saucepan on the stovetop over medium-low heat, make the sauce by melting the butter. Add the garlic and sauté for 1 to 2 minutes. Add the wine, lemon juice, and hot sauce. Season with salt and pepper to taste. Simmer for 5 minutes. Remove the saucepan from the heat and stir in the parsley. Keep warm.

3. Discard any mussels that are cracked or don't snap shut when tapped. Place the mussels in a large aluminum foil roasting pan and cover tightly with heavy-duty aluminum foil.

4. Place the pan on the grate and steam the mussels until the shells open, about 10 to 12 minutes. Remove the pan from the grill and use long-handled tongs to remove the foil from the pan. (Be careful of escaping steam.) Use the tongs to discard any mussels that don't open.

5. Pour the reserved garlic butter sauce over the mussels. Serve from the pan or transfer the mussels to a shallow serving bowl. Serve immediately with lemon wedges, additional hot sauce, and crusty bread (if using) to sop up the juices.

Teriyaki Smoked Honey Tilapia

Servings: 4

Cooking Time: 120 Minutes

Ingredients:

- 4 tilapia fillets
- 1 cup teriyaki sauce
- 2/3 cup honey
- 1 tbsp sriracha sauce
- Green onions (optional)

Directions:

1. In a large bowl, make the marinade by mixing together the teriyaki sauce, honey,and sriracha. Make sure honey is dissolved and well blended.

2. Place the tilapia fillets in the marinade. Turn the fillets so they are completely coated. Cover with a plastic wrap and marinate in the fridge for about 2 hours.

3. Supply your smoker with wood pellets and follow the start-up procedure. Preheat the grill, with the lid closed, to 275° F.

4. Remove the tilapia fillets from the marinade and transfer them to the grill. Smoke the fillets until they reach an internal temperature of 145°F, about 2 hours.

5. Sprinkle with green onions if desired.

Hot-smoked Salmon

Servings: 4

Cooking Time: 180minutes

Ingredients:

- 1½lb (680g) skinless center-cut salmon fillet, preferably wild caught
- for the brine
- 1 quart (1 liter) distilled water
- ¼ cup coarse salt
- ¼ cup light brown sugar or low-carb equivalent
- ¼ cup gin (optional)

Directions:

1. In a saucepan on the stovetop over medium-high heat, make the brine by combining the water, salt, brown sugar, and gin (if using). Bring the mixture to a boil. Stir until the salt and sugar dissolve. Remove the pan from the stovetop and let the brine cool to room temperature. Refrigerate until cool.

2. Run your fingers over the salmon fillet, feeling for bones. Remove any with kitchen tweezers or needle-nosed pliers. Rinse the salmon under cold running water. Place the salmon in a resealable plastic bag and pour the brine over it. Refrigerate for 4 to 8 hours.

3. Place a wire rack on a rimmed sheet pan. Remove the salmon from the brine and rinse under cold running water. Pat dry with paper towels and then place the salmon on the wire rack. Place the pan in a cool area with good air

circulation (such as near a fan). In 2 to 4 hours, you'll notice the salmon has developed a pellicle—a kind of sticky skin or coating that will help the smoke adhere to the fish. (Don't skip this step.)

4. Supply your smoker with wood pellets and follow the start-up procedure. Preheat the grill, with the lid closed, to 150° F.

5. Place the salmon on the grate and smoke until the fish flakes easily when pressed with a fork and the internal temperature reaches 140°F (60°C), about 3 hours. If albumin (a harmless white protein) appears on top of the fillet as it smokes, gently remove it with a paper towel.

6. Remove the salmon from the grill and let rest for 10 minutes. (You can also transfer the fish to a clean wire rack and let it cool to room temperature. Cover and refrigerate if not using immediately. The salmon will keep for up to 5 days.)

7. Serve the salmon with eggs, on salads, with Mustard Caviar, or with its traditional accompaniments: cream cheese, capers, chopped hard-boiled eggs, diced red onion, and dark bread.

Pacific Northwest Salmon

Servings: 4
Cooking Time: 75 Minutes

Ingredients:

- 1 (2-pound) half salmon fillet
- 1 batch Dill Seafood Rub
- 2 tablespoons butter, cut into 3 or 4 slices

Directions:

1. Supply your smoker with wood pellets and follow the start-up procedure. Preheat the grill, with the lid closed, to 180°F.

2. Season the salmon all over with the rub. Using your hands, work the rub into the flesh.

3. Place the salmon directly on the grill grate, skin-side down, and smoke for 1 hour.

4. Place the butter slices on the salmon, equally spaced. Increase the grill's temperature to 300°F and continue to cook until the salmon's internal temperature reaches 145°F. Remove the salmon from the grill and serve immediately.

Citrus-smoked Trout

Servings: 6
Cooking Time: 120 Minutes

Ingredients:

- 6 to 8 skin-on rainbow trout, cleaned and scaled
- 1 gallon orange juice
- ½ cup packed light brown sugar
- ¼ cup salt
- 1 tablespoon freshly ground black pepper
- Nonstick spray, oil, or butter, for greasing
- 1 tablespoon chopped fresh parsley
- 1 lemon, sliced

Directions:

1. Fillet the fish and pat dry with paper towels.

2. Pour the orange juice into a large container with a lid and stir in the brown sugar, salt, and pepper.

3. Place the trout in the brine, cover, and refrigerate for 1 hour.

4. Cover the grill grate with heavy-duty aluminum foil. Poke holes in the foil and spray with cooking spray (see Tip).

5. Supply your smoker with wood pellets and follow the start-up procedure. Preheat, with the lid closed, to 225°F.

6. Remove the trout from the brine and pat dry. Arrange the fish on the foil-covered grill grate, close the lid, and smoke for 1 hour 30 minutes to 2 hours, or until flaky.

7. Remove the fish from the heat. Serve garnished with the fresh parsley and lemon slices.

Mezcal Shrimp With Salsa De Molcajete

Servings: 4

Cooking Time: 14 Minutes

Ingredients:

- 18 to 24 jumbo shrimp, about 1½lb (680g) total, peeled and deveined
- ⅓ cup mezcal
- juice of ½ lime
- 2 tbsp extra virgin olive oil
- 2 tsp coarse salt
- 1 tsp ground cumin
- lime wedges
- for the salsa
- 2 Roma tomatoes
- 2 tomatillos, husked and washed
- 2 garlic cloves, peeled and impaled on a toothpick
- 1 jalapeño or serrano pepper
- 1 small white onion, halved
- ½ tsp coarse salt, plus more
- juice of ½ lime
- ¼ cup loosely packed fresh cilantro leaves

Directions:

1. Supply your smoker with wood pellets and follow the start-up procedure. Preheat the grill, with the lid closed, to 450° F.

2. In a large bowl, combine the shrimp, mezcal, lime juice, olive oil, salt, and ground cumin. Toss with your hands to mix thoroughly. Set aside for 15 minutes and then toss once more.

3. Begin to make the salsa by placing the tomatoes, tomatillos, garlic, jalapeño, and onion on the grate. Grill until they begin to char, about 3 minutes for the garlic and about 6 to 8 minutes for the other vegetables, turning as needed. Transfer the vegetables to a rimmed sheet pan. Remove the skewers from the garlic. Let everything cool. Coarsely chop the vegetables and leave them in separate piles.

4. Place the garlic in the molcajete and add the salt. Mash the garlic to a purée using the temolote. Add the onion and grind it into the garlic paste. Stir in the jalapeño (deseeded for a milder salsa), tomatoes, and tomatillos. Stir in the lime juice and cilantro leaves. Taste, adding salt. (If you don't own a molcajete or temolote, prepare the salsa using a small food processor.)

5. Drain the shrimp and discard the marinade. Thread the shrimp on wood or bamboo skewers. Place the shrimp on the grate and grill until they're white and opaque, about 4 to 6 minutes, tossing with tongs.

6. Transfer the shrimp to a platter. Serve with the salsa and lime wedges.

Dijon-smoked Halibut

Servings: 6

Cooking Time: 120 Minutes

Ingredients:

- 4 (6-ounce) halibut steaks
- ¼ cup extra-virgin olive oil
- 2 teaspoons kosher salt
- 1 teaspoon freshly ground black pepper
- ½ cup mayonnaise
- ½ cup sweet pickle relish

- ¼ cup finely chopped sweet onion
- ¼ cup chopped roasted red pepper
- ¼ cup finely chopped tomato
- ¼ cup finely chopped cucumber
- 2 tablespoons Dijon mustard
- 1 teaspoon minced garlic

Directions:

1. Rub the halibut steaks with the olive oil and season on both sides with the salt and pepper. Transfer to a plate, cover with plastic wrap, and refrigerate for 4 hours.

2. Supply your smoker with wood pellets and follow the start-up procedure. Preheat, with the lid closed, to 200°F.

3. Remove the halibut from the refrigerator and rub with the mayonnaise.

4. Put the fish directly on the grill grate, close the lid, and smoke for 2 hours, or until opaque and an instant-read thermometer inserted in the fish reads 140°F.

5. While the fish is smoking, combine the pickle relish, onion, roasted red pepper, tomato, cucumber, Dijon mustard, and garlic in a medium bowl. Refrigerate the mustard relish until ready to serve.

6. Serve the halibut steaks hot with the mustard relish.

Grilled Albacore Tuna With Potato-tomato Casserole

Servings: 8
Cooking Time: 20 Minutes

Ingredients:
- 6 Tuna Steaks, 6oz
- 1 Whole lemon zest
- 1 chile de árbol, thinly sliced
- 1 Tablespoon thyme
- 1 Tablespoon fresh parsley

Directions:

1. To make the fish: Season the fish with the lemon zest, chile, thyme, and parsley. Cover and refrigerate at least 4 hours.

2. Remove fish from the refrigerator 30 minutes before cooking to come to room temperature.

3. Season the fish with salt and pepper on both sides. Grill 2-3 minutes per side (next to the cast iron with the casserole) rotating it once or twice. The tuna should be well seared but still rare.

Kimi's Simple Grilled Fresh Fish

Servings: 2
Cooking Time: 45 Minutes

Ingredients:
- 1 Cup soy sauce
- 1/3 Cup extra-virgin olive oil
- 1 Tablespoon garlic, minced
- 2 lemons, juiced
- fresh basil
- 4 Pound Fresh Fish, cut into portion-sized pieces

Directions:

1. Mix all ingredients to create sauce and cover fish in marinade for 45 minutes.

2. Supply your smoker with wood pellets and follow the start-up procedure. Preheat the grill, with the lid closed, to 140° F. Grill the marinated fish on the grill until it reaches an internal temperature of 140-145°F. Serve immediately, enjoy! Grill: 350 °F Probe: 145 °F

Grilled Lemon Salmon

Servings: 4
Cooking Time: 60 Minutes

Ingredients:

- Dill, Fresh
- 1 Lemon, Sliced
- 1 1/2 - 2 Lbs Salmon, Fresh

Directions:

1. Supply your smoker with wood pellets and follow the start-up procedure. Preheat the grill, with the lid closed, to 225° F.
2. Place the salmon on a cedar plank. Lay the lemon slices along the top of the salmon. Smoke in your Grill for about 60 minutes.
3. Top with fresh dill and serve.

Roasted Halibut With Spring Vegetables

Servings: 4
Cooking Time: 20 Minutes

Ingredients:

- 4 thick-cut halibut fillets
- 2 Tablespoon Fin & Feather Rub
- Butcher Paper
- 1 Pound Carrots, Peeled and Cut into 3/4" Inch Slices
- 1 Pound asparagus, ends trimmed
- 1/2 Pound Oyster Mushrooms
- 2 Tablespoon butter
- salt and pepper
- 1/2 Cup white wine

Directions:

1. Season the halibut fillets with Traeger Fin and Feather Rub.
2. To build the packets: Start with four sheets of parchment paper about twenty inches long. Fold in half, then open it back up.
3. Divide the carrots, asparagus, and mushrooms between the four pieces of parchment and top each with a little bit of butter. Season with salt and pepper. Place a halibut fillet on top of the vegetables in each packet.
4. Next, fold the paper over so the two ends meet, enclosing the food. Beginning at either end of the center crease, make small, overlapping diagonal folds around the filling, sealing the packet tight. Before finishing the final fold, pour a little bit of wine in each packet then seal completely.
5. Supply your smoker with wood pellets and follow the start-up procedure. Preheat the grill, with the lid closed, to 500° F.
6. Place all four packets on a sheet tray and place in the grill. Cook for 7-10 minutes or until the internal temperature of the fish reaches 145°F. Remove from the grill and place packet on a serving dish. Grill: 500 °F Probe: 145 °F
7. Using a knife or scissors, cut open each packet and fold the edges back. Finish with a little bit of lemon juice if desired. Enjoy!

Flavour Fire Spiced Shrimp

Servings: 2
Cooking Time: 8 Minutes

Ingredients:

- 1 pound of extra large raw whole wild shrimp
- 1 tablespoon vegetable oil
- 1 tablespoon chili powder
- 1 teaspoon garlic powder
- 1/2 teaspoon onion powder
- 1/2 teaspoon cayenne pepper

- 1/4 teaspoon paprika
- 1/4 teaspoon dried oregano
- Pinch of Kosher salt

Directions:

1. Supply your smoker with wood pellets and follow the start-up procedure. Preheat the grill, with the lid closed, to High heat.

2. While grill is preheating, remove the shrimp shells, leaving the heads.

3. Butterfly shrimp by using a knife to cut each shrimp down the middle, from the head down to the tail.

4. Remove the vein, rinse off the shrimp and lightly dry off with paper towels.

5. Place the shrimp in a large bowl, sprinkle with all the seasonings and the oil.

6. Mix together, ensuring the mixture evenly covers each shrimp.

7. Using a skewer, impale the whole body of a shrimp, from head to tail. (Wrap them in aluminum foil if using wooden skewers).

8. Place the whole shrimp on the grill and cook for 3-4 minutes on each side (Or until shells turns pink and the shrimp is opaque).

9. Serve with your favorite sauce or condiment.

Prosciutto-wrapped Scallops

Servings: 4
Cooking Time: 10 Minutes

Ingredients:

- 1½lb (680g) jumbo sea or diver scallops (size U-10)
- 8 to 10 thin slices of prosciutto, each halved lengthwise
- coarse salt
- freshly ground black pepper
- for the butter
- 8oz (225g) unsalted butter
- 2 tsp minced fresh curly or flat-leaf parsley
- 1½ tsp finely grated orange zest
- 1 tbsp freshly squeezed orange juice
- 1 tsp finely grated lemon zest
- 1 tsp finely grated lime zest
- ½ tsp coarse salt

Directions:

1. Supply your smoker with wood pellets and follow the start-up procedure. Preheat the grill, with the lid closed, to 450° F.

2. In a small saucepan on the stovetop over medium-low heat, make the citrus butter by melting the butter. Add the remaining ingredients and simmer for 3 to 5 minutes to blend the flavors. Keep warm.

3. Rinse the scallops under cold running water and dry with paper towels. Place each scallop on its side at the end of a piece of prosciutto and wrap the prosciutto around the scallop. Secure with a toothpick. Season the exposed sides of the scallop with salt and pepper.

4. Place the scallops exposed sides down on the grate and grill until the edges of the prosciutto begin to frizzle and the scallop is warm inside, about 3 to 5 minutes per side.

5. Transfer the scallops to a platter. Brush with some of the warm citrus butter before serving. Serve the remaining butter on the side.

BAKING RECIPES

Baked Buttermilk Biscuits

Servings: 4
Cooking Time: 15 Minutes

Ingredients:
- 2 Cup all-purpose flour
- 1/4 Cup butter
- 3/4 Cup buttermilk

Directions:
1. Supply your smoker with wood pellets and follow the start-up procedure. Preheat the grill, with the lid closed, to High heat. Spoon the flour into a measuring cup and level with a knife.
2. Put the flour into a mixing bowl. Using a pastry blender, cut the butter into the flour until the mixture resembles coarse crumbs.
3. With a fork, gently stir in just enough of the buttermilk so the dough leaves the sides of the bowl. (You may not need all the buttermilk.) For the most tender biscuits, do not overmix.
4. Lightly flour a work surface as well as your hands. Tip the dough onto the floured surface and gently bring together using your fingertips. (Re-flour your hands or the board if the dough is too sticky.) Knead two or three times, just to bring the dough together.
5. With a floured rolling pin, lightly and quickly roll the dough out to a thickness of about 1/2". Using a 1-1/2" floured cutter, cut out as many biscuits as you can. (Do not twist the cutter; push it straight down.) You can reroll the scraps if desired, but the "second string" biscuits will be tougher.
6. Transfer the biscuits to an ungreased baking sheet. Using a pastry brush, brush the tops with melted butter. Bake until golden brown, 10 to 15 minutes. Enjoy! Grill: 500 °F

Pizza Bites

Servings: 6
Cooking Time: 20 Minutes

Ingredients:
- 4 1/2 Cup Bread Flour
- 1 1/2 Tablespoon sugar
- 2 Teaspoon Instant Yeast
- 2 Teaspoon kosher salt
- 3 Tablespoon extra-virgin olive oil
- 15 Fluid Ounce Water, Lukewarm
- 8 Ounce Pepperoni, sliced
- 1 Cup pizza sauce
- 1 Cup mozzarella cheese
- 1 Whole egg, for egg wash
- 1 As Needed salt

Directions:
1. For the Pizza Dough: Combine flour, sugar, salt, and yeast in food processor. Pulse 3 to 4 times until incorporated evenly. Add olive oil and water. Run food processor until mixture forms ball that rides around the bowl above the blade, about 15 seconds. Continue processing 15 seconds longer.
2. Transfer dough ball to lightly floured surface and knead once or twice by hand until smooth ball is formed. Divide dough into three even parts and place each into a 1 gallon zip top bag. Place in refrigerator and allow to rise at least one day.
3. At least two hours before baking, remove dough from refrigerator and shape into balls by gathering dough towards bottom and pinching shut. Flour well and place each one in a separate

medium mixing bowl. Cover tightly with plastic wrap and allow to rise at warm room temperature until roughly doubled in volume.

4. When ready to cook, set the grill temperature to 350°F and preheat, lid closed for 15 minutes.

5. After the first rise remove the dough from the fridge and let come to room temperature. Roll dough on a flat surface. Cut dough into long strips 3" wide by 18" long.

6. Slice pepperoni into strips.

7. In a medium bowl combine the pizza sauce, mozzarella and pepperoni.

8. Spoon 1 TBSP of the pizza filling onto the pizza dough every two inches, about halfway down the length of the dough. Dip a pastry brush into the egg wash and brush around pizza filling. Fold the half side of the dough (without the pizza filling) over the other the half that contains the pizza filling.

9. Press down between each pizza bite slightly with your fingers. With a ravioli or pizza cutter, cut around each filling- creating a rectangle shape and sealing the crust in.

10. Transfer each pizza bite onto a parchment lined cookie sheet. Cover with a kitchen towel and let them rise for 30 minutes.

11. When ready to cook, preheat the grill to 350 ℉ with the lid closed for 10-15 minutes.

12. Brush the bites with remaining egg wash, sprinkle with salt and place directly on the sheet tray. Bake 10-15 minutes until the exterior is golden brown.

13. Remove from grill and transfer to a serving dish. Serve with extra pizza sauce for dipping and enjoy!

Grilled Beer Cheese Dip

Servings: 6
Cooking Time: 20 Minutes

Ingredients:
- 6 Oz Beer, Can
- 8 Oz Cream Cheese
- 1 Tsp Onion Powder
- ½ Tsp Pepper
- ½ Tsp Salt
- 2 Cups Shredded Cheese

Directions:

1. Supply your smoker with wood pellets and follow the start-up procedure. Preheat the grill, with the lid closed, to 350° F. If you're using a gas or charcoal grill, set it up for medium high heat. Preheat with lid closed for 10-15 minutes.

2. In the cast iron pan add cream cheese, shredded cheese, beer, onion powder, salt and pepper. Once grill is at 350°F place cast iron skillet onto the grill and cook for about 10 minutes, stir and cook for another 5-10 minutes.

3. Top with more shredded cheese and fresh parsley. Serve with fresh baked pretzels as well.

Old Fashioned Cornbread

Servings: 4
Cooking Time: 25 Minutes

Ingredients:
- 1 Cup all-purpose flour
- 1 Cup Cornmeal
- 1 Tablespoon sugar
- 2 Teaspoon baking powder
- 1/2 Teaspoon salt
- 3 Tablespoon butter
- 1 Cup milk
- 1 Whole egg, lightly beaten

Directions:

1. In a mixing bowl, combine the flour, cornmeal, sugar, baking powder, and salt.

2. Melt the butter in a small saucepan. Remove from the heat, and stir in the milk and the egg. (Make sure the mixture isn't hot or the egg will curdle.)

3. Add the milk-egg mixture to the dry ingredients and stir to combine. Do not overmix.

4. Spread the batter evenly in a greased 8 or 9-inch square baking pan or pie plate.

5. Supply your smoker with wood pellets and follow the start-up procedure. Preheat the grill, with the lid closed, to 375° F.

6. Bake the cornbread until it begins to pull away from the sides of the pan and the top is beginning to brown, 25 to 35 minutes. Cut into squares (or wedges, if you used a pie plate) for serving. Grill: 375 °F

Vanilla Chocolate Bacon Cupcakes

Servings: 12
Cooking Time: 120 Minutes

Ingredients:

- 1 Lb Bacon
- 1 1/2 Tsp Baking Powder
- 1 1/2 Tsp Baking Soda
- 1 Cup Cocoa, Powder
- 2 Egg
- 1 3/4 Cups Flour
- 1 Cup Milk, Whole
- 1/2 Cup Oil
- 1 Tsp Salt
- 2 Cups Sugar
- 2 Tsp Vanilla

Directions:

1. Supply your smoker with wood pellets and follow the start-up procedure. Preheat the grill, with the lid closed, to 250° F.

2. Once your grill is preheated, place bacon strips on the grates. Smoke for 1hr-1 ½ hours or until desired crispiness is achieved.

3. Remove the bacon from the grill and set aside.

4. Increase set the temperature to 350°F and preheat.

5. Mix the rest of the ingredients in a bowl with an electric mixer until it is nice and smooth.

6. Pour the mixture into a cupcake tin.

7. Transfer the tin to your grill and bake for about 20 - 25 minutes.

8. Allow the cupcakes to cool on a wire rack. Once cooled, top with your favorite premade icing and a half of strip of the bacon. Serve and enjoy!

Delicious Pellet Grill Cornbread

Servings: 6
Cooking Time: 35 Minutes

Ingredients:

- 1 cup flour
- 1 cup cornmeal
- 2 teaspoons baking powder
- 2 teaspoons salt
- 3/4 cup sugar
- 2 tablespoons honey
- 1/2 cup butter
- 1 cup sour cream
- 3 eggs
- 1 cup milk

Directions:

1. Supply your smoker with wood pellets and follow the start-up procedure. Preheat the grill, with the lid closed, to 350° F.

2. Grease a 12-inch cast iron skillet or an equivalent baking pan.

3. Add flour, cornmeal, baking powder, salt, sugar, honey, butter, sour cream, eggs, and milk into a mixing bowl.

4. Mix well then pour into pan and bake on the grill for 30-35 minutes or until the cornbread is baked through in the center.

Bananas Rum Foster

Servings: 4
Cooking Time: 10 Minutes

Ingredients:
- 1/3 Cup Banana Nectar
- 4 Bananas, Quartered
- 3/4 Cup Brown Sugar
- 1/4 Cup Butter
- 1/2 Tsp Cinnamon, Ground
- 1/3 Cup Dark Rum
- Vanilla Ice Cream

Directions:
1. Supply your smoker with wood pellets and follow the start-up procedure. Preheat the grill, with the lid closed, to medium heat. If using a gas or charcoal grill, preheat a cast iron skillet.

2. Place a large skillet on the griddle, then melt butter in the skillet. Whisk in brown sugar and cinnamon, stirring until sugar dissolves.

3. Add the banana nectar and bananas. Stir to coat

4. Once the bananas begin to soften and turn brown, add the rum. Stir, then ignite the sauce with a stick lighter. After the flames subside, simmer the sauce for 2 minutes.

5. Divide the bananas among 4 scoops/bowls of vanilla ice cream, then spoon the warm sauce over the top of the ice cream. Serve immediately.

Vanilla Chocolate Chip Cookies

Servings: 12
Cooking Time: 20 Minutes

Ingredients:
- 3/4 cup brown sugar
- 3/4 cup white sugar
- 1 stick butter, room temp
- 2 eggs
- 1 tsp vanilla
- 2 1/2 cups flour
- 1/2 tsp salt
- 1 tsp baking soda
- 1 cup Chocolate Chips

Directions:
1. Cream your butter and sugar together in a mixing bowl using a hand mixer or stand mixer on medium speed for about 4-5 minutes.

2. Once the butter is creamed, add the eggs and vanilla. Continue mixing for an additional minute.

3. Put flour, salt, and baking soda in a sifter. Sift it into your creamed butter mixture.

4. Scrape the sides of your mixing bowl with a rubber spatula, and then turn your mixer on to low speed.

5. Let it mix a little, and then scrape the sides again. Stop mixing when there are one or two streaks of flour left in the cookie dough.

6. Scrape the sides of your bowl and pour in a cup of chocolate chips, and turn the mixer to low again to mix the chocolate. It should take just a few turns for the chocolate pieces to be well incorporated.

7. Line a large baking sheet with parchment paper. Using a medium cookie scoop (about 1.5 tbsp), drop evenly spaced dollops of cookie dough onto the cookie sheet.

8. Supply your smoker with wood pellets and follow the start-up procedure. Preheat the grill, with the lid closed, to 350° F. Place the cookie sheet in your smoker, and let them cook for about 12 minutes.

9. Let them sit on a cooling rack while you continue to cook the additional cookies.

10. Cool for a few minutes to let cookies set.

11. Enjoy!

Crème Brûlée

Servings: 2
Cooking Time: 45minutes

Ingredients:

- 1 Quart heavy whipping cream
- 1 Pieces Vanilla Bean, split and scraped
- 6 Large egg yolk
- 1 Cup sugar

Directions:

1. Supply your smoker with wood pellets and follow the start-up procedure. Preheat the grill, with the lid closed, to 325° F.

2. Pour the cream into a saucepan over medium-high heat, add the vanilla bean and the scraped seeds. Bring to a boil. Remove from the heat and allow to steep (about 15 minutes). Remove the vanilla bean from saucepan and discard.

3. In a bowl, whisk together egg yolks and 1/2 cup (100 g) of the sugar until the mix starts to lighten in color. Add the cream a little at a time, stirring continually.

4. Pour the mixture into 6 (8 oz) ramekins and place the ramekins into a large roasting pan. Pour hot water into the pan so that it comes halfway up the sides of the ramekins.

5. Place water bath pan on the grill and bake until the Crème Brûlées still jiggle in the center, about 40 to 45 minutes. Grill: 325 °F

6. Remove the ramekins from the roasting pan and refrigerate for at least 2 hours and up to 2 days.

7. To serve, let the Crème Brûlée come to temperature (about 20 minutes) before torching the tops.

8. Sprinkle the remaining 1/2 cup (100 g) sugar equally on top of each ramekin. Using a torch in a circular motion, melt the sugar until it caramelizes and forms a crispy top.

9. Allow the Crème Brûlée to sit for a few minutes before serving. Enjoy!

Irish Soda Bread

Servings: 8-12
Cooking Time: 45 Minutes

Ingredients:

- As Needed Cornmeal
- 3 1/2 Cup all-purpose flour
- 1 1/2 Teaspoon sugar
- 1 1/4 Teaspoon baking soda
- 1 Teaspoon salt
- 1 Cup buttermilk
- To Taste butter

Directions:

1. When ready to cook, set the temperature to 400F (205 C) and preheat, lid closed, for 10 to 15 minutes.

2. Lightly dust the bottom of an 8-inch (20-cm) round cake pan with cornmeal and set aside.

3. Tear off a large sheet of wax paper and lay it on your work surface.

4. Combine the flour, sugar, soda, and salt in a large sifter and sift onto the wax paper. Carefully

lift up the sides of the wax paper and tip the flour mixture back into the sifter. Re-sift into a large mixing bowl.

5. Lightly flour your work surface. Make a well in the middle of the flour mixture in the bowl and pour in 1 cup (240 mL) of buttermilk. Stir with a wooden spoon. Work quickly and gently as the carbon dioxide bubbles formed when the buttermilk hits the dry ingredients will deflate, the dough will look somewhat shaggy. If the dough seems dryish, add a little more buttermilk.

6. Turn out onto the floured surface, and with floured hands, knead gently for 10 to 20 seconds - just long enough to bring the dough bits together. (It will look more like biscuit dough than bread dough.)

7. Form into a flattish round and transfer to the prepared pan. Flour a sharp knife, and deeply cut a cross in the top of the loaf all the way to the edge of the bread. Quickly get it in to bake, if it sits too long, it will deflate.

8. Bake the bread for 45 to 50 minutes, or until it is browned and the bottom of the loaf sounds hollow when rapped with your knuckles.

9. Remove the bread from the baking pan and cool on a cooling rack. Just be-fore serving, cut the loaf in half and then slice each half into thin slices.

10. Serve with butter. Wrap leftovers tightly in plastic wrap or foil. This bread makes great toast. Enjoy!

Baked Pear Tarte Tatin

Servings: 6
Cooking Time: 45 Minutes

Ingredients:
- 2 1/2 Cup all-purpose flour
- 2 Tablespoon sugar
- butter chilled
- 8 Tablespoon cold water
- 1/4 Cup granulated sugar
- 1/4 Cup butter
- 8 Whole Bartlett Pear

Directions:
1. Supply your smoker with wood pellets and follow the start-up procedure. Preheat the grill, with the lid closed, to 350° F.

2. For the crust: Place flour and sugar in a food processor and pulse to mix. Add butter a little at a time while pulsing. Once it starts to looks like cornmeal, add the water until dough start to come together.

3. Form a round with the dough, wrap in plastic and let it cool in the refrigerator.

4. While dough cools, make the caramel sauce. In a sauce pan, add 1/4 cup granulated sugar and 1/4 cup butter. Cook butter and sugar until it becomes a dark caramel, a couple minutes.

5. Pour caramel in the bottom of 10 inch deep cake pan. While the caramel is still hot, arrange pear wedges in a fan formation covering the caramel.

6. Roll the chilled pie dough into a circle big enough to cover the pan. Prick the pie dough with a fork and cover the pan with the pie dough. Trim the crust leaving room for shrinkage.

7. Place on the grill and bake for 45 minutes or until pears are soft. The pears will be soft and most of the juice will evaporate and thicken.

8. Let sit for 3 minutes. While pan is still hot, place a plate over pie and flip over. Slowly lift the plate.

9. Serve warm, topped with vanilla ice cream or whipped cream. Enjoy!

Blueberry Bread Pudding

Servings: 4
Cooking Time: 60 Minutes

Ingredients:

- 5 eggs
- 3 Cup sugar
- 2 1/2 Cup milk
- 1 1/2 Teaspoon vanilla
- 1 Teaspoon cinnamon
- 1 Pinch salt
- 5 Cup Bread
- 3 Cup blueberries

Directions:

1. Beat the eggs in a large mixing bowl. Whisk in the sugar, milk, vanilla, cinnamon, and salt.
2. In another large bowl, combine the bread and 2 cups (200 g) of the blueberries.
3. Pour the egg mixture over the bread-blueberry mixture and let sit for 30 minutes. Meanwhile, place muffin liners in a muffin tin.
4. Supply your smoker with wood pellets and follow the start-up procedure. Preheat the grill, with the lid open.
5. Spoon the bread-blueberry mixture into the prepared cups; evenly top each with the remaining cup of blueberries, pressing them gently into the pudding with the back of a spoon.
6. Dust the top with sugar.
7. Arrange the pan directly on the grill grate and smoke for 30 minutes. Grill:180°F
8. Increase the temperature to 350F (180 C), and bake until the pudding is set and golden brown on top, about 25 minutes. Grill:350°F
9. Let cool slightly, then sift powdered sugar on top. Serve warm with sweetened whipped cream or vanilla ice cream, if desired.

Savory Cheesecake With Bourbon Pecan Topping

Servings: 6
Cooking Time: 75 Minutes

Ingredients:

- Crust
- 12 ounce Oreos
- 6 ounce melted butter
- Filling
- 24 ounces cream cheese - room temperature
- 1 cup granulated sugar
- 3 tbs cornstarch
- 2 large eggs
- 2/3 cup heavy cream
- 1 tbs vanilla
- 1 1/2 tbs bourbon
- Topping
- 3 large eggs beaten
- 1/3 cup granulated sugar
- 1/3 cup brown sugar
- 8 tbsp corn syrup dark corn syrup recommended
- 2 tbsp bourbon
- 1/2 tbsp vanilla
- 1/8 tbsp salt
- 3/4 cup rough chopped pecans (smoked pecans recommended)

Directions:

1. Supply your smoker with wood pellets and follow the start-up procedure. Preheat the grill, with the lid closed, to 350 °F.
2. Wrap foil on the bottom and up the sides of a 9" spring-form pan (outside of pan).
3. Butter the bottom & insides of the pan.
4. Crust

5. Throw ingredients in a food processor until they are finely ground.

6. Spread in 9" cheesecake pan on bottom & about ½ way upsides.

7. Filling

8. Place 8 oz of cream cheese in mixer bowl with 1/3 of sugar & cornstarch.Mix until smooth andcreamy.

9. Add another 8 oz cream cheese andbeat until smooth, then add remaining cream cheese,beating until smooth.

10. Then mix in the rest of the sugar, bourbon & vanilla.

11. Add eggs one at a time beating well after each one.

12. Add the heavy cream and mix just until smooth. Reminder: Do not over mix.

13. Pour batter into the prepared crust.

14. Topping

15. Mix all together except pecans.

16. Sprinkle pecans on top of cheesecake batter.

17. Pour topping over cheesecake batter.

18. Place in a pan big enough to hold a spring-form pan. Pour boiling water in the roasting pan to come up about ½ way up the spring-form pan.

19. Bake at 350 °F for 75 minutes until the top just barely jiggles. Carefully take the pan out of water-bath and put on cooling rack.

20. Let cool for 2 hours in pan. After 2 hours put in fridge until totally chilled then serve.

Focaccia

Servings: 6
Cooking Time: 40 Minutes

Ingredients:
- 1 Cup warm water (110°F to 115°F)
- 1/2 Ounce Yeast, active
- 1 Teaspoon sugar
- 2 1/2 Cup flour
- 1 Teaspoon salt
- 1/4 Cup extra-virgin olive oil
- 1 1/2 Teaspoon Italian herbs, dried
- 1/8 Teaspoon red pepper flakes
- As Needed coarse sea salt

Directions:

1. Measure the water in a glass-measuring cup. Stir in the yeast and sugar. Let rest for in a warm place. After 5 to 10 minutes, the mixture should be foamy, indicating the yeast is "alive." If it does not foam, discard it and start again.

2. Pour the water/yeast mixture in the bowl of a food processor. Add 1 cup of the flour as well as the salt and 1/4 cup of olive oil. Pulse several times to blend. Add the remaining flour, Italian herbs, and hot pepper flakes.

3. Process the dough until it's smooth and elastic and pulls away from the sides of the bowl, adding small amounts of flour or water through the feed tube if the dough is respectively too wet or too dry.

4. Let the dough rise in the covered food processor bowl in a warm place until doubled in bulk, about 1 hour5. Remove the dough from the food processor (it will deflate) and turn onto a lightly floured surface.

5. Oil two 8- to 9-inch round cake pans generously with olive oil. (Just pour a couple of glugs in and tilt the pan to spread the oil.) Divide the dough into two equal pieces, shape into disks, and put one in each prepared cake pan.

6. Oil the top of each disk with olive oil and dimple the dough with your fingertips. Sprinkle lightly with coarse salt, and if desired, additional dried Italian herbs.

7. Cover the focaccia dough with plastic wrap and let the dough rise in a warm place, about 45 minutes to an hour.

8. When ready to cook, start the smoker grill and set the temperature to 400F and preheat, lid closed, for 10 to 15 minutes.

9. Put the pans with the focaccia dough directly on the grill grate. Bake until the focaccia breads are light golden in color and baked through, 35 to 40 minutes, rotating the pans halfway through the baking time.

10. Let cool slightly before removing from the pans. Cut into wedges for serving.

Bacon Chocolate Chip Cookies

Servings: 2
Cooking Time: 10-12 Minutes

Ingredients:

- 2¾ cups all-purpose flour
- 1½ teaspoons baking soda
- ½ teaspoon salt
- 12 tablespoons (1½ sticks) unsalted butter, softened
- 1 cup light brown sugar
- 1 cup granulated sugar
- 2 eggs, at room temperature
- 2½ teaspoons apple cider vinegar
- 1 teaspoon vanilla extract
- 2 cups semisweet chocolate chips
- 8 slices bacon, cooked and crumbled

Directions:

1. In a large bowl, combine the flour, baking soda, and salt, and mix well.

2. In a separate large bowl, using an electric mixer on medium speed, cream the butter and sugars. Reduce the speed to low and mix in the eggs, vinegar, and vanilla.

3. With the mixer speed still on low, slowly incorporate the dry ingredients, chocolate chips, and bacon pieces.

4. Supply your smoker with wood pellets and follow the start-up procedure. Preheat, with the lid closed, to 375°F.

5. Line a large baking sheet with parchment paper.

6. Drop rounded teaspoonfuls of cookie batter onto the prepared baking sheet and place on the grill grate. Close the lid and smoke for 10 to 12 minutes, or until the cookies are browned around the edges.

Smoked Sweet Beer Bread

Servings: 6
Cooking Time: 60 Minutes

Ingredients:

- 3 cups all-purpose flour, sifted
- 2 tbsp. sugar
- 1 tbsp. baking powder
- 1 tsp. salt
- 1 (12 oz) can or bottle beer (not too dark or bitter)
- 2 tbsp. honey or agave, warmed
- 6 tbsp. butter, melted

Directions:

1. Supply your smoker with wood pellets and follow the start-up procedure. Preheat the grill, with the lid closed, to 350° F.

2. Lightly grease a 9 ×5 inch loaf pan.

3. In a large mixing bowl, put in the flour, sugar, baking powder, and salt. Whisk to combine and aerate, using a wire whisk. Add the beer and honey and stir with a wooden spoon until the batter is properly mixed (Do not over-mix).

4. Pour half of the melted butter into the prepared loaf pan and pour in the batter. Pour the remaining butter over the top of the loaf.

5. Place the loaf pan on the grill grate and bake for 50 to 60 minutes or until the bread is golden brown.

6. Allow the loaf to cool slightly in the pan before removing it from the pan. Leftovers make great toast.

Baked Parker House Rolls

Servings: 8

Cooking Time: 15 Minutes

Ingredients:
- 1/2 Ounce (2 packets) active dry yeast
- 6 Tablespoon plus 1 teaspoon cane sugar
- 1 Cup warm water (110°F to 115°F)
- 5 Cup all-purpose flour, plus more as needed
- 2 Teaspoon salt
- 1 Cup warm milk (110°-115°F)
- 1 Large eggs
- oil
- 4 Tablespoon melted butter, divided
- 1 Tablespoon Maldon Sea Salt Flakes
- 2 Tablespoon poppy seeds
- 2 Tablespoon white sesame seeds
- 1 Tablespoon garlic flakes

Directions:
1. Place the yeast, 1 teaspoon of cane sugar and warm water in a mixing bowl or the base of a stand mixer. Stir to combine. Allow the yeast to proof for 5 minutes- it should start to bubble a bit, showing that the yeast is alive.

2. Sprinkle the flour, salt and remaining 6 tablespoons of sugar over the yeast mixture. Using a dough hook or a wooden spoon, stir for 30 seconds. Pour in the warm milk and egg.

3. Knead again on the medium-low setting, or on a floured work surface by hand until the dough is very soft, adding up to one more cup of flour so the dough is soft and smooth and has lost its sticky quality.

4. Coat the bowl with a small film of oil and place the dough in the bowl, turning to coat dough evenly with the oil. Cover the bowl with a clean cloth, place in a warm spot in the kitchen and allow to proof about 45 minutes. The dough will almost double in size.

5. Punch down the dough and place on a floured work surface. Divide the dough in half, then divide each half into 12 equal pieces.

6. Using your hands, tuck in the seams of each piece of dough then place the dough on a lightly floured surface.

7. Place your fingers around the piece of dough, and roll it in a circular motion to create a smooth, even ball. Alternately, roll the dough between your two hands to create a round ball shape. Repeat with the remaining 23 pieces.

8. Butter a 9x13 inch baking pan with a tablespoon of the melted butter. Place the dough balls evenly in the pan, creating rows of 4 pieces of dough across and 6 down. Cover again with a clean towel and allow the dough to rise in a warm spot, about 30 minutes longer.

9. While the dough is proofing, supply your smoker with wood pellets and follow the start-up procedure. Preheat the grill, with the lid closed, to 325° F. Brush the remaining 3 tablespoons of butter on the bread and sprinkle with the flake salt, seeds and garlic flakes.

10. Place the pan on the grill, cover and bake about 15 to 20 minutes, or until rolls are lightly browned on top and cooked through. When done, you should be able to pull apart two pieces and see that the dough is cooked and the bottoms are lightly browned. Grill: 325 °F

Baked Bourbon Maple Pumpkin Pie

Servings: 6-8

Cooking Time: 60 Minutes

Ingredients:

- 1/4 Cup Cocoa Powder, Unsweetened
- 1 Tablespoon Cocoa Powder, Unsweetened
- 3 1/2 Tablespoon sugar
- 1 Teaspoon salt
- 1 1/4 Cup all-purpose flour
- 1 Tablespoon all-purpose flour
- 6 Tablespoon butter
- 2 Tablespoon vegetable oil
- 1 Large Egg Yolk
- 1/2 Teaspoon apple cider vinegar
- 1/4 Cup ice water
- 1 Large egg, beaten
- 15 Ounce Pumpkin, canned
- 1/4 Cup sour cream
- 2 Tablespoon bourbon
- 1 Teaspoon ground cinnamon
- 1/2 Teaspoon salt
- 1/4 Teaspoon ground ginger
- 1/4 Teaspoon ground nutmeg
- 1/8 Teaspoon Allspice, ground
- 1/8 Teaspoon Mace, ground
- 3 Large eggs
- 3/4 Cup maple syrup
- 2 Tablespoon sugar
- 1/2 Vanilla Bean, halved
- 1 Cup heavy cream

Directions:

1. For the Chocolate Pie Dough: Pulse cocoa powder, granulated sugar, salt, and 1-1/4 cups plus 1 Tbsp flour in a food processor to combine. Add butter and shortening and pulse until mixture resembles coarse meal with a few pea-sized pieces of butter remaining. Transfer to a large bowl.

2. Whisk together the egg yolk, vinegar, and 1/4 cup ice water in a small bowl. Drizzle half of the egg mixture over flour mixture and, using a fork, mix gently just until combined. Add remaining egg mixture and mix until the dough just comes together (you will have some unincorporated pieces).

3. Turn out dough onto a lightly floured surface, flatten slightly, and cut into quarters. Stack pieces on top of one another. Placing unincorporated dry pieces of dough between layers, and press down to combine. Repeat process twice more (all pieces of dough should be incorporated at this point). Form dough into a 1" thick disk. Wrap in plastic; chill at least 1 hour.

4. Roll out a disk of dough on a lightly floured surface into a 14" round. Transfer to a 9" pie dish. Lift up the edge and allow the dough to slump down into the dish. Trim. Leaving about 1" overhang. Fold overhang under and crimp edge. Chill in freezer 15 minutes.

5. When ready to cook, set the smoker to 350°F and preheat, lid closed for 15 minutes.

6. Line pie with parchment paper or heavy-duty foil, leaving a 1-1/2" overhang. Fill with pie weights or dried beans. Bake until crust is dry around the edge, about 20 minutes.

7. Remove paper and weights and bake until surface of the crust looks dry, 5-10 minutes.

8. Brush bottom and sides of crust with 1 beaten egg. Return to grill and bake until dry and set, about 3 minutes longer.

9. For the Pumpkin Maple Filling: Whisk together pumpkin puree, sour cream, bourbon,

cinnamon, salt, ginger, nutmeg, allspice, mace (optional) and remaining 3 eggs in a large bowl; set aside.

10. Pour maple syrup and 2 tbsp sugar in a small saucepan. Scrape in the seeds from vanilla bean (reserve pod for another use) or add vanilla extract and bring syrup to a boil. Reduce heat to medium-high and simmer, stirring occasionally, until mixture is thickened and small puffs of steam start to release about 3 minutes.

11. Remove from heat and add cream in 3 additions, stirring with a wooden spoon after each addition until smooth. Gradually whisk hot maple cream into pumpkin mixture.

12. Place pie dish on a rimmed baking sheet and pour in pumpkin filling. Bake pie, rotating halfway through, until set around edge but center barely jiggles 50-60 minutes.

13. Transfer pie dish to a wire rack and let the pie cool. Slice and serve. Enjoy!

Chili Cheese Fries

Servings: 6
Cooking Time: 10 Minutes

Ingredients:
- 1 Cup Cheddar Cheese, Shredded
- 1 Cup Chili Con Carne, Prepared
- 1 Bag French Fries
- 1 Tablespoon Olive Oil
- 1 Tablespoon Sweet Heat Rub

Directions:

1. Supply your smoker with wood pellets and follow the start-up procedure. Preheat the grill, with the lid closed, to 350° F. If you're using charcoal or gas, set it up for medium high heat.

2. Bake the fries according to manufacturer's instructions. Once the fries are done, place them in a large bowl and add the olive oil and Sweet Heat Rub. Toss the fries to coat. Once everything is well coated with the oil and seasoning, spread the fries on a baking sheet.

3. Top the fries with the chili and the shredded cheddar cheese. Place the baking sheet on the grill and grill for 7-10 minutes, or until the cheese is melted and bubbly, and the chili is warm all the way through.

4. Remove the baking sheet from the grill and serve the fries immediately.

Quick Baked Dinner Rolls

Servings: 8
Cooking Time: 30 Minutes

Ingredients:
- 2 Tablespoon quick-rise yeast
- 1 Teaspoon salt
- 1/4 Cup sugar
- 3 1/3 Cup flour
- 1/4 Cup unsalted butter, softened
- 1 egg
- cooking spray
- 1 egg, for egg wash

Directions:

1. Combine yeast and warm water in a small bowl to activate the yeast. Let sit until foamy, about 5-10 minutes.

2. Combine salt, sugar, and flour in the bowl of a stand mixer fitted with the dough hook. Pour water and yeast into the dry ingredients with the machine running on low.

3. Add butter and egg and mix for 10 minutes gradually increasing the speed from low to high.

4. Form the dough into a ball and place in a buttered bowl. Cover with a cloth and let the dough rise for approximately 40 minutes.

5. Transfer the risen dough to a lightly floured surface and divide into 8 pieces forming a ball with each.

6. Lightly spray a cast iron pan with cooking spray and arrange balls in the pan. Cover with a cloth and let rise 20 minutes.

7. Supply your smoker with wood pellets and follow the start-up procedure. Preheat the grill, with the lid closed, to 375° F.

8. Brush rolls with egg wash and then bake for 30 minutes until lightly browned. Serve hot. Enjoy! Grill: 375 ˚F

Sweet Cheese Muffins

Servings: 3
Cooking Time: 15 Minutes

Ingredients:

- 1 package butter cake mix
- 1 package Jiffy Corn Muffin Mix
- 1 cup self-rising or cake flour
- 12 tablespoons (1½ sticks) unsalted butter, softened, plus 8 tablespoons (1 stick) melted
- 3½ cups shredded Cheddar cheese
- 2 eggs, beaten, at room temperature
- 2¼ cups buttermilk
- Nonstick cooking spray or butter, for greasing
- ¼ cup packed brown sugar

Directions:

1. Supply your smoker with wood pellets and follow the start-up procedure. Preheat, with the lid closed, to 375°F.

2. In a large mixing bowl, combine the cake mix, corn muffin mix, and flour.

3. Slice the 1½ sticks of softened butter into pieces and cut into the dry ingredients. Add the cheese and mix thoroughly.

4. In a medium bowl, combine the eggs and buttermilk, then add to the dry ingredients, stirring until well blended.

5. Coat three 12-cup mini muffin pans with cooking spray and spoon ¼ cup of batter into each cup.

6. Transfer the pans to the grill, close the lid, and smoke, monitoring closely, for 12 to 15 minutes, or until the muffins are lightly browned.

7. While the muffins are cooking, make the topping: In a small bowl, stir together the remaining 1 stick of melted butter and the brown sugar until well combined.

8. Remove the muffins from the grill. Brush the tops with the sweet butter and serve warm.

Tarte Tatin

Servings: 6
Cooking Time: 55 Minutes

Ingredients:

- 2 Cup all-purpose flour
- 1 Teaspoon salt
- 1 Cup butter
- 5 Tablespoon cold water
- 1/4 Cup unsalted butter
- 3/4 Cup granulated sugar
- 10 Granny Smith Apples, Cut Into Wedges

Directions:

1. Supply your smoker with wood pellets and follow the start-up procedure. Preheat the grill, with the lid closed, to 350° F.

2. For the crust: Place flour and salt in a food processer and pulse to mix. Add butter a little at a time while pulsing. Once it starts to looks like cornmeal, add the water until dough start to come together. Form a round with the dough, wrap in plastic and let it cool in the refrigerator.

3. While dough cools, place a pie dish or a 10-inch round cake pan on the grill; add butter and sugar to pie dish. Let it caramelize.

4. When the sugar caramelizes and has come to a dark amber color, take off grill. Arrange apple wedges in a fan formation covering the caramel.

5. Roll the pie crust into a circle big enough to cover the pan. Prick the pie dough with a fork and cover the pan with the pie dough. Trim the crust leaving room for shrinkage.

6. Place on the grill and bake for 55 minutes until apples are soft. Let sit for 3 minutes. While pan is still hot, place a plate over pie and flip over. Grill: 350 °F

7. Serve warm, topped with ice cream or whipped cream. Enjoy!

Chocolate Peanut Cookies

Servings: 4
Cooking Time: 12 Minutes

Ingredients:
- 1/2 Tsp Baking Soda
- 1/2 Cup Brown Sugar
- 1/2 Cup + 1 Tbsp Butter, Unsalted
- 1/3 Cup Cocoa Powder, Dark And Unsweetened
- 2 Eggs, Beaten
- 1 1/2 Cups Flour, All-Purpose
- 1/3 Cup Miniature Chocolate Chips
- 2 Cups Peanut Butter Chips, Divided
- 1/4 Tsp Sea Salt
- 1/2 Cup Sugar, Granulated
- 1 Tsp Vanilla Extract

Directions:
1. Supply your smoker with wood pellets and follow the start-up procedure. Preheat the grill, with the lid closed, to medium-low heat. If using a gas or charcoal grill, preheat a cast iron skillet.

2. In a mixing bowl, whisk together the flour, cocoa powder, baking soda, and salt. Set aside.

3. Set a metal saucepan on the griddle, then add ½ cup of butter to melt. Whisk in the sugars and vanilla extract and cook for 2 minutes. Remove the pan from the griddle, and transfer contents to a large mixing bowl.

4. Slowly pour the beaten eggs into the sugar mixture, whisking constantly to temper the eggs.

5. Add the dry mixture to the wet ingredients until just combined. Fold in 1 cup of peanut butter chips and chocolate chips. Refrigerate mixture for 15 to 30 minutes.

6. Remove the dough from the refrigerator, then add an additional cup of peanut butter chips.

7. Portion dough into 16 to 18 cookie balls.

8. Melt 1 tablespoon of butter on the griddle, then transfer the cookie balls to the griddle. Press down gently on the cookies, then cook for 10 to 12 minutes, flipping halfway.

9. Transfer cookies to a cooling rack for 5 minutes before enjoying.

Green Bean Casserole Circa 1955

Servings: 6
Cooking Time: 30 Minutes

Ingredients:
- 1 1/2 Pound Green Beans, fresh
- 1 Can cream of mushroom soup
- 1/2 Cup milk
- 2 Teaspoon soy sauce
- 1/2 Teaspoon Worcestershire sauce
- 1/2 Teaspoon black pepper
- 1.334 Cup French's Original Crispy Fried Onions

- 1/4 Cup red bell pepper, diced

Directions:

1. In a mixing bowl, combine the beans (trimmed and cooked until tender, or may use 2 16 oz. cans), soup, milk, soy sauce, Worcestershire sauce, black pepper, 2/3 cup of the onion rings, and red pepper, if using. Transfer to a 1-1/2 quart casserole dish.

2. Supply your smoker with wood pellets and follow the start-up procedure. Preheat the grill, with the lid closed, to 375° F.

3. Cook the casserole until the filling is hot and bubbling, 25 to 30 minutes. Top with the remaining onions and cook for 5 to 10 minutes more, or until the onions are crisp and beginning to brown. Grill: 375 °F

Rosemary Cranberry Apple Sage Stuffing

Servings: 7
Cooking Time: 45 Minutes

Ingredients:
- 10 Cups Day Old Diced Bread, Sliced Loaf
- 2 1/2 Cups Broth, Chicken
- 1 Cup Butter, Unsalted
- 1 Cup Diced Celery, Cut
- 1 1/2 Cups Fresh Cranberries
- 1 Beaten Egg
- 1 Medium Granny Smith Apple, Peel, Core And Dice
- 2 Tbsp Minced Parsley, Fresh
- 1 Tbsp Minced Rosemary, Fresh
- 2 Tbsp Roughly Chopped Sage
- Salt And Pepper
- 1 Tbsp Minced Thyme
- 2 Cups Diced Yellow Onion, Sliced

Directions:

1. Supply your smoker with wood pellets and follow the start-up procedure. Preheat the grill, with the lid closed, to 350° F.

2. Melt butter over medium heat. Add onions then celery and cook until onions start to become translucent.

3. In a large bowl, mix together bread, apples, cranberries, cooked onion and celery mixture, and fresh herbs.

4. Add half of the chicken broth to the mixture and stir.

5. Beat together eggs and the rest of the chicken broth in a small bowl. Pour into the bread mixture and stir until completely combined.

6. Add salt and pepper to taste.

7. Pour stuffing into a cast iron pan or baking dish. Cover with foil and bake on the grill for 30 minutes. Remove the foil and cook for an additional 15 minutes.

8. Serve immediately and enjoy!

Sweet And Spicy Baked Pork Beans

Servings: 20
Cooking Time: 120 Minutes

Ingredients:
- 1 - 21 Oz Apple Pie Filling, Can
- 1 Gallon Baked Beans
- 1 Tbs Chilli, Powder
- 1 Green Bell Pepper, Diced
- 1 10 Oz Drained Jalapeno, Can Diced
- 1 Cup Maple Syrup
- 1 Onion, Diced
- 1 Lb Pork, Pulled

Directions:

1. Supply your smoker with wood pellets and follow the start-up procedure. Preheat the grill, with the lid closed, to 350° F.

2. Place all ingredients in mixing bowl and mix well.

3. Pour bean mixture into foil pans.

4. Bake in grill till bubbling throughout – about 2 hours.

5. Rest at least 15 minutes before serving.

Strawberry Basil Daiquiri

Servings: 2

Cooking Time: 20 Minutes

Ingredients:
- 4 strawberries, stemmed
- 6 Tablespoon granulated sugar, divided
- 6 basil leaves
- 3 Ounce white rum
- 2 Ounce lime juice
- 1 Ounce Smoked Simple Syrup
- 2 fresh basil leaves, for garnish
- 2 lime slice, for garnish

Directions:

1. Supply your smoker with wood pellets and follow the start-up procedure. Preheat the grill, with the lid closed, to 375° F.

2. Cut strawberries in half and coat in 2 tablespoons granulated sugar. Place directly on grill grate and cook for 15 to 20 minutes. Remove from heat and cool. Grill: 375 °F

3. Add 1 tablespoon granulated sugar and basil leaves to shaking tin and lightly muddle. Add strawberries and muddle again.

4. Pour in white rum, lime juice and Smoked Simple Syrup. Shake with ice.

5. Strain contents into a chilled glass and garnish with large fresh basil leaf and sliced lime. Enjoy!

Cast Iron Pineapple Upside Down Cake

Servings: 6

Cooking Time: 40 Minutes

Ingredients:
- 1/4 Cup butter, melted
- 1 Cup brown sugar
- 20 Ounce Pineapple, sliced
- 6 Ounce maraschino cherries
- 1 Whole Yellow Cake Mix, Boxed
- vegetable oil
- eggs

Directions:

1. Supply your smoker with wood pellets and follow the start-up procedure. Preheat the grill, with the lid closed, to 350° F.

2. Pour melted butter into a 12-inch cast iron pan. Sprinkle brown sugar on top of the butter. Arrange pineapple slices on brown sugar, squeezing in as many slices as possible. Place a cherry in center of each pineapple slice; press gently into brown sugar.

3. Make cake batter as directed on box, substituting pineapple juice mixture for as much of the water as possible, and adding in required oil and eggs. Pour batter into cast iron dish, over pineapple and cherries.

4. Place the cast iron pan on the grill grate and cook for 20 minutes. Rotate the pan a half turn to ensure it cooks evenly. Cook for an additional 20 minutes, or until toothpick inserted in center comes out clean.

5. Immediately run knife around side of pan to loosen cake. Place heatproof serving plate upside down onto pan; turn plate and pan over.

6. Leave pan over cake 5 minutes so brown sugar topping can drizzle over cake. Cool 30 minutes. Enjoy!

Blueberry Pancakes

Servings: 4

Cooking Time: 10 Minutes

Ingredients:

- 2 Cups Blueberries, Fresh
- 1 Cup Pancake Mix
- 1/2 Cup Sugar
- 3/4 Cup Water, Warm

Directions:

1. Supply your smoker with wood pellets and follow the start-up procedure. Preheat the grill, with the lid closed, to 350° F.

2. Place the cast iron griddle on the grates of your grill.

3. In a large bowl, pour water, pancake mix and 1/2 cup of the blueberries and mix until combined.

4. Pour the batter onto the griddle in 4 equal parts. Cook with the lid closed for about 6 minutes, or until the edges of the pancakes are slightly cooked. Flip each pancake and continue cooking for another 4 minutes.

5. Pour the hot blueberry sauce over your freshly cooked pancakes and enjoy!

PORK RECIPES

Triple Threat Pork Fattywith Stuffed Jalapeños

Servings: 10

Cooking Time: 150 Minutes

Ingredients:

- 16 strips of bacon, about 1¼lb (565g) total, not thick cut
- 1½ tsp Tajin seasoning, plus more
- 8oz (225g) light cream cheese, at room temperature
- 3 large jalapeños, decored, destemmed, and deseeded
- 1lb (450g) seasoned breakfast sausage
- 1lb (450g) ground pork
- 6 to 8oz (170 to 225g) thinly sliced pepper Jack cheese

Directions:

1. Supply your smoker with wood pellets and follow the start-up procedure. Preheat the grill, with the lid closed, to 275° F.

2. Moisten a workspace with a damp towel. Place a 15-inch (38cm) rectangle of plastic wrap on the workspace. Place 8 strips of bacon, sides touching, parallel to the edge of the plastic. Fold back the even-numbered strips at the halfway point and place a 9th snugly against the folds (perpendicular to the first 8). Unfold.

3. Fold back the odd-numbered strips and place a 10th snugly against the folds. Unfold. Repeat until the weave is complete. Place another sheet of plastic over the weave. Use a rolling pin to thin and tighten the weave.

4. In a small bowl, combine the Tajin and cream cheese. Tightly stuff each jalapeño with the mixture. Reserve any extra filling.

5. Place the sausage and pork in a large bowl. Wet your hands with cold water and knead the meats to combine. Transfer to a resealable plastic bag. Use a rolling pin to create a rectangle that's smaller than the dimensions of your bacon weave. (For reference, place the weave alongside the bag.) Slit the sides of the bag to release the meat and then position the bag over the weave and remove the remaining plastic.

6. Cover the meat with the pepper Jack, leaving 1 inch (2.5cm) around the edges. Pipe the reserved cream cheese mixture randomly over the surface. Position the stuffed jalapeños end to end on the long side of the meat. Use the plastic under the weave to tightly roll up the fatty from the side with the jalapeños. Use bamboo skewers to secure the weave. Lightly season the outside with more Tajin seasoning.

7. Place the fatty seam side down on the grate and smoke until the internal temperature reaches 160°F (71°C), about 2 to 2½ hours.

8. Transfer the fatty to a cutting board and let rest for 10 minutes. Use an electric knife to slice the fatty into 1-inch (2.5cm) rounds before serving.

Balsamic Brussels Sprouts With Bacon

Servings: 8

Cooking Time: 25 Minutes

Ingredients:

- 6 Strips thick-cut bacon

- 2 Pound Brussels sprouts, trimmed and halved
- 1 Small onion, diced
- 2 Tablespoon olive oil or vegetable oil
- freshly ground black pepper
- salt
- 1/2 Cup chicken stock
- 1 Tablespoon balsamic vinegar

Directions:

1. Supply your smoker with wood pellets and follow the start-up procedure. Preheat the grill, with the lid closed, to 450° F.

2. Place the bacon strips directly on the grill grate and cook for 20 minutes. Grill: 450 ℉

3. Line a large baking sheet with foil for easy cleanup. Place the onion and sprouts cut-side down on the baking sheet, drizzle with oil and season with salt and pepper.

4. Place the baking sheet directly on the grill grate next to the bacon and roast until they turn a light golden brown, about 8 to 10 minutes. Grill: 450 ℉

5. Add the cooked bacon, pour chicken stock and balsamic vinegar over the sprouts, mix and continue to cook until the liquid has thickened. Remove from heat. Enjoy!

Grilled Prosciutto Wrapped Asparagus

Servings: 6
Cooking Time: 15 Minutes

Ingredients:

- 2 Bunch asparagus
- 4 Ounce prosciutto
- olive oil
- salt and pepper
- 1 Medium lemon, zested
- 2 Tablespoon balsamic vinegar, divided
- 3 Tablespoon toasted pine nuts, for serving

Directions:

1. Supply your smoker with wood pellets and follow the start-up procedure. Preheat the grill, with the lid closed, to 400° F.

2. Rinse the asparagus and pat dry with a paper towel. Cut the bottom third off of the asparagus stalks and discard.

3. Wrap a piece of prosciutto around 4 to 5 stalks, and place on a baking sheet. Drizzle the asparagus with olive oil, then sprinkle with salt, pepper and lemon zest.

4. Place the baking sheet on the grill and cook. After 5 minutes, shake the pan to turn the asparagus once, then drizzle with 1 tablespoon balsamic vinegar. Grill: 400 ℉

5. Place back on the grill and cook until the prosciutto is crispy and the asparagus is cooked through, about 5 to 8 minutes. Grill: 400 ℉

6. Place the asparagus on the serving tray and sprinkle with the pine nuts and drizzle with remaining balsamic. Enjoy!

Hawaiian Pineapple Pork Butt

Servings: 8 - 10
Cooking Time: 720 Minutes

Ingredients:

- 6 - 8 Pineapple Rings
- 2 Cups Pineapple, Juice
- 1 8-10Lb Pork Butt Roast, Bone-In
- ¼ Cup Sweet Heat Rub

Directions:

1. Supply your smoker with wood pellets and follow the start-up procedure. Preheat the grill, with the lid open, to 225° F. If not using a pellet smoker, set up the smoker for indirect smoking.

2. Remove the pork butt from its packaging and drain any excess liquid from the pork butt. Pat the pork butt dry with paper towels and discard the paper towels.

3. Generously season the pork butt with the Sweet Heat seasoning, making sure that the roast is coated on all sides.

4. Place the pineapple rings evenly over the pork shoulder, fat side up, and pin with toothpicks. Place the pork butt into the 9x13 pan and pour the pineapple juice over the top.

5. Set the pan into the smoker. Make sure that the pork butt is placed as close to the center of the rack as possible for even cooking.

6. Place a temperature probe into the thickest part of the pork butt, and smoke the pork until it reaches an internal temperature of 201°F. The pork should be deeply browned and smell very porky.

7. Once the pork butt reaches its internal temperature, remove the pork butt from the grill and wrap it tightly in foil. Allow the roast to rest for at least 1 hour before shredding.

8. After the roast has rested for an hour, shred the pork with your meat claws, discarding any large chunks of fat. Serve immediately.

Bacon Stuffed Onion Rings

Servings: 6
Cooking Time: 120 Minutes

Ingredients:
- 1 Pack Bacon
- 2 White Onions

Directions:
1. Supply your smoker with wood pellets and follow the start-up procedure. Preheat the grill, with the lid open, to 250° F.

2. Peel each onion and cut into thirds, separating the onion slices into rings. Using two slices of bacon, wrap around the onion ring until the ring is fully covered, securing in place with a toothpick. Continue until all the bacon is used up.

3. Place the onion rings on the and smoke until the bacon is cooked, about 120 minutes.

Prosciutto Wrapped Dates With Marcona Almonds

Servings: 8
Cooking Time: 5 Minutes

Ingredients:
- 24 Whole medjool dates
- 1 Small container Marcona salted almonds
- 8 Ounce prosciutto
- 2 Tablespoon olive oil
- 2 limes, washed and dried for zesting
- honey, for serving
- flake salt, for serving

Directions:
1. Supply your smoker with wood pellets and follow the start-up procedure. Preheat the grill, with the lid closed, to 400° F.

2. Place a large cast iron pan into the grill to preheat. Using a small paring knife, cut a slit lengthwise across the top of each date. Remove the pit. Replace pits with 1 to 2 Marcona almonds, then press the dates back together with your fingers to seal.

3. Cut the prosciutto into 24 pieces lengthwise. To wrap each date, place one at the bottom of a strip of prosciutto, then roll the prosciutto around the date to cover, leaving a little bit of the date showing on each end.

4. Add 2 Tablespoons olive oil to the preheated cast iron pan. Place the dates in the pan and cook,

searing the prosciutto on all sides, turning as needed, about 3 to 5 minutes total. When the prosciutto is crispy, carefully remove the pan from the grill.

5. Zest the limes over the pan so the citrus zest is absorbed into the olive oil and onto the dates. Place the dates on a serving platter. Sprinkle with flake salt, an additional drizzle of olive oil, honey and serve. Enjoy!

Bacon Wrapped Asparagus

Servings: 4
Cooking Time: 20 Minutes

Ingredients:

- 1 Bunch asparagus
- 1 Tablespoon olive oil
- 1/2 Teaspoon garlic powder
- 1/2 Teaspoon onion powder
- salt and pepper
- 1 Pound Bacon, sliced

Directions:

1. Coat the Asparagus evenly with olive oil, then sprinkle the asparagus evenly with, garlic powder, onion powder, salt and pepper. Individually wrap each asparagus with 1 piece of thin cut bacon.
2. Supply your smoker with wood pellets and follow the start-up procedure. Preheat the grill, with the lid closed, to 450° F.
3. Place the wrapped asparagus on the grill and roast for 15-20 minutes, or until the bacon is crispy. Enjoy!

Traeger Roasted Easter Ham

Servings: 8
Cooking Time: 60 Minutes

Ingredients:

- 1 (6-7 lb) bone-in ham

- 1 Cup Sweet & Heat BBQ Sauce
- 2 Cup brown sugar
- 1/2 Cup pineapple juice

Directions:

1. Supply your smoker with wood pellets and follow the start-up procedure. Preheat the grill, with the lid closed, to 225° F.
2. Place ham in grill and cook for 60 minutes. Grill: 225 °F
3. While the ham is cooking, mix together the Traeger Sweet & Heat BBQ Sauce, brown sugar and pineapple juice.
4. Glaze ham with the sauce every 10 minutes during the last 30 minutes. Remove ham from grill and serve. Enjoy!

3-2-1 Spare Ribs

Servings: 4
Cooking Time: 180 Minutes

Ingredients:

- 2 racks of St. Louis–cut pork spare ribs, each about 3lb (1.4kg)
- all-purpose barbecue rub
- 3 tbsp unsalted butter, cut into cubes
- 1 cup apple juice or apple cider
- low-carb barbecue sauce

Directions:

1. Supply your smoker with wood pellets and follow the start-up procedure. Preheat the grill, with the lid closed, to 225° F.
2. Place the ribs on a rimmed sheet pan and dust with the rub. Place the ribs bone side down on the grate and smoke for 3 hours.
3. Tear off 2 large sheets of heavy-duty aluminum foil. Place one rack of ribs bone side down on the foil and top with half the butter cubes. Place the second rack of ribs bone side

down on the butter cubes and top with the remaining butter cubes.

4. Bring up all 4 sides of the foil and pour in the apple juice. Crimp the edges of the foil so the ribs are tightly enclosed. Place the foil package on the grate and smoke for 2 hours more.

5. Transfer the ribs to a workspace and carefully open the foil package. (Be careful of escaping steam.) Discard the foil and any accumulated juices. Brush the ribs on both sides with barbecue sauce. Place the ribs on the grate and smoke for 1 hour more to set the sauce and firm up the bark.

6. Transfer the ribs to a cutting board. Use a sharp knife to cut the slabs in half or into individual ribs. Serve immediately.

Traeger Cajun Broil

Servings: 8
Cooking Time: 60 Minutes

Ingredients:
- 2 Tablespoon olive oil
- 2 Pound red potatoes
- Old Bay Seasoning
- 6 Corn Ears, each cut into thirds
- 2 Pound smoked kielbasa sausage
- 3 Pound large shrimp with tails, deveined
- 2 Tablespoon butter

Directions:
1. Supply your smoker with wood pellets and follow the start-up procedure. Preheat the grill, with the lid closed, to 450° F.

2. Drizzle potatoes with half of the olive oil and lightly season with Old Bay seasoning. Place directly on the grill grate. Roast 20 minutes or until tender. Grill: 450 ˚F

3. Drizzle corn with remaining olive oil and lightly season with Old Bay seasoning. Place corn

and kielbasa directly on the grill grate next to the potatoes. Roast 15 minutes. Grill: 450 ˚F

4. Season shrimp with Old Bay seasoning. Place shrimp directly on grill grate next to the rest of the items and cook for 10 minutes, or until bright pink and cooked through. Grill: 450 ˚F

5. Remove everything from the grill and transfer to a large bowl. Add butter and season with more Old Bay seasoning to taste. Toss to coat and serve immediately. Enjoy!

Grilled Lemon Pepper Pork Tenderloin

Servings: 4
Cooking Time: 20 Minutes

Ingredients:
- 2 lemons, zested
- 1 Clove garlic, minced
- 1 Teaspoon freshly minced parsley
- 1 Teaspoon lemon juice
- 1/4 Teaspoon black pepper
- 1/2 Teaspoon kosher salt
- 2 Tablespoon olive oil
- 1 (2 lb) pork tenderloin

Directions:
1. In a small bowl, whisk together everything except the tenderloin.

2. Trim all silverskin and excess fat from the tenderloin.

3. Place pork in a large resealable bag. Pour the marinade over the tenderloin and zip closed. Transfer to the refrigerator and marinate for at least 2 hours but no more than 8.

4. Supply your smoker with wood pellets and follow the start-up procedure. Preheat the grill, with the lid closed, to 375° F.

5. Remove the tenderloin from the bag and discard the marinade.

6. When the grill is hot, place tenderloin directly on the grill grate and cook 15 to 20 minutes, flipping once halfway through until the internal temperature reaches 145°F. Grill: 375 °F Probe: 145 °F

7. Remove from the heat and let rest 5 to 10 minutes before slicing. Enjoy!

Maple Syrup Bacon Wrapped Tenderloin

Servings: 5
Cooking Time: 30 Minutes

Ingredients:
- 1 Package Bacon, Thick Cut
- 1/4 Cup Maple Syrup
- 2 Tbsp Olive Oil
- 3 Tbsp Competition Smoked Rub
- 1 Trimmed With Silver Skin Removed Pork, Tenderloin

Directions:
1. Lay the strips of bacon out flat, with each strip slightly overlapping the other.

2. Sprinkle the pork tenderloin with 1 tablespoon of the Competition Smoked Rub and lay in the center.

3. Wrap with bacon over the tenderloin and tuck in the ends.

4. In a small bowl, mix the olive oil, maple syrup and remaining seasoning together and brush onto the wrapped tenderloin.

5. Supply your smoker with wood pellets and follow the start-up procedure. Preheat the grill, with the lid open, to 350° F.

6. When the grill is ready, place your tenderloin on the grill and cook, turning, for 15 minutes.

7. Increase the grill temperature to 400°F and grill for another 15 minutes or until the internal temperature is 145°F. Serve and enjoy!

Spiced Coffee-rubbed Ribs

Servings: 6 - 8
Cooking Time: 360 Minutes

Ingredients:
- 1 Tbsp Ancho Chili Powder
- Ground Black Pepper
- ½ Tsp Cocoa Powder
- 2 Tbsp Coffee
- ½ Tsp Coriander, Ground
- 1 Tbsp Dark Brown Sugar
- 1 Tsp Garlic Powder
- 2 Tbsp Kosher Salt
- 1 Tsp Onion Powder
- 1 Tsp Oregano
- 2 Tbsp Paprika
- 8 Lbs. Pork Spareribs

Directions:
1. Begin by preparing the dry rub. In a mixing bowl, whisk together the coffee, salt, paprika, brown sugar, oregano, garlic powder, onion powder, black pepper, cocoa powder and coriander. Set aside.

2. Remove the membrane from the back of your ribs: Take a butter knife and wedge it just underneath the membrane to loosen it. Using your hands or a paper towel to grip, pull the membrane up and off the bone. Place the ribs on a sheet tray, then rub each rack generously with dry rub. Wrap ribs in foil, then refrigerate overnight.

3. When ready to cook, remove ribs from the refrigerator and let come to room temp. Supply your smoker with wood pellets and follow the

start-up procedure. Preheat the grill, with the lid open, to 225° F. If using a gas or charcoal grill, set it up for low indirect heat.

4. Place foil-wrapped ribs on the grill and close lid. Cook for 4 hours then remove foil from ribs and pour accumulated juices into a glass measuring cup. Pour the sauce over the ribs, then continue to cook for an additional 1 ½ - 2 hours or until tender. Remove from grill, slice and serve.

Pickle Brined Grilled Pork Chops

Servings: 4
Cooking Time: 60 Minutes

Ingredients:
- 4 pork chops
- 3 Cup Dill Pickle Brine, jar
- coarse ground black pepper, divided

Directions:
1. Put the pork chops and pickle brine in a resealable plastic bag. Refrigerate for at least 4 hours. Drain well and pat dry with paper towels.
2. Season generously with black pepper.
3. Supply your smoker with wood pellets and follow the start-up procedure. Preheat the grill, with the lid closed, to 300° F.
4. Put the chops directly on the grill grate and grill, turning once, for about 1 hour, or until the internal temperature of the chop is at least 145°F. Grill: 300 °F Probe: 145 °F
5. Let rest for 5 minutes before serving. Enjoy!

Jamaican Jerk Pork Chops

Servings: 4
Cooking Time: 720 Minutes

Ingredients:
- 4 thick pork rib or loin chops, each about 12oz (340g) and 1 inch (2.5cm) thick
- for the marinade
- ½ to 1 Scotch bonnet or habanero pepper, destemmed, deseeded, and coarsely chopped, plus more
- 2 scallions, trimmed, white and green parts coarsely chopped
- 1 garlic clove, peeled and coarsely chopped
- juice of 1 lime
- 2 tbsp vegetable oil
- 2 tbsp distilled water
- 1 tbsp light soy sauce
- 2 tsp coarsely chopped fresh thyme leaves
- 2 tsp peeled and minced fresh ginger
- 2 tsp dark brown sugar or low-carb substitute, plus more
- 1 tsp coarse salt, plus more
- ½ tsp freshly ground black pepper
- ½ tsp ground allspice
- ½ tsp ground nutmeg
- ½ tsp ground cinnamon

Directions:
1. In a blender, make the jerk marinade by combining the ingredients. Blend until fairly smooth. Taste for seasoning, adding more Scotch bonnet, brown sugar, or salt. Place the pork chops in a resealable plastic bag and pour the marinade over them, turning and massaging the bag to thoroughly coat the meat. Refrigerate for 2 to 4 hours.
2. Supply your smoker with wood pellets and follow the start-up procedure. Preheat the grill, with the lid closed, to 425° F.
3. Remove the pork from the marinade and scrape off the excess. (Discard the marinade.) Grill the chops until the internal temperature reaches 145°F (63°C), about 6 to 8 minutes per side.
4. Transfer the chops to a platter. Let rest for 2 minutes before serving.

Bacon-draped Injected Pork Loin Roast

Servings: 4
Cooking Time: 180 Minutes

Ingredients:

- 1 Cup apple juice
- 1/4 Cup water
- 1 Teaspoon salt
- 1 Teaspoon Worcestershire sauce
- 3 Pound (3 lb) center-cut pork loin
- Sweet Rub
- 10 Slices bacon

Directions:

1. In a small bowl combine apple juice, water, salt, and Worcestershire; stir to dissolve the salt crystals.Plunge the injector into the sauce and retract the needle to draw up the liquid. Liberally inject the meat.
2. Plunge the injector into the sauce and retract the needle to draw up the liquid. Liberally inject the meat.
3. Season the meat all over with the Traeger Sweet Rub.
4. Supply your smoker with wood pellets and follow the start-up procedure. Preheat the grill, with the lid closed, to 225° F.
5. Drape the loin with the bacon slices. Put the roast directly on the grill grate and smoke for 3 to 4 hours, or until the internal temperature of the meat is at least 145 degrees F on an instant-read thermometer. Grill: 225 ˚F Probe: 145 ˚F
6. Transfer the pork to a cutting board and let rest for 10 minutes before carving and serving. Enjoy!

Crown Roast Of Pork

Servings: 4
Cooking Time: 60 Minutes

Ingredients:

- 1 Whole Crown Roast of Pork, 12-14 ribs
- 1/4 Cup Pork & Poultry Rub
- 1 Cup apple juice
- 1 Cup Apricot BBQ Sauce

Directions:

1. Supply your smoker with wood pellets and follow the start-up procedure. Preheat the grill, with the lid closed, to 375° F.
2. Season the pork roast liberally with Traeger Pork and Poultry Rub. Let sit at room temperature for 30 minutes. Wrap each tip of the crown roast in a small piece of aluminum foil. This will protect the bones during the cook and prevent them from turning black.
3. Place the roast directly on the grill grate and cook for about 90 minutes spraying with apple juice every 30 minutes or so.
4. When the roast reaches an internal temperature of 125 degrees F, remove the aluminum foil from the bones and return to the grill.
5. Spray again with apple juice and continue to cook until the internal temperature reaches 135 degrees F in the thickest part of the roast. In the last ten minutes, baste the roast with the Apricot BBQ Sauce to let the glaze set.
6. Remove from the grill, tent with foil, and let it rest 15-20 minutes before slicing. Enjoy!

Orange & Maple Baked Ham

Servings: 2
Cooking Time: 120 Minutes

Ingredients:

- 2/3 Cup orange juice
- 1/3 Cup maple syrup
- 1/3 Cup Marmalade, Orange
- 1/8 Cup Dijon mustard
- 1 1/3 Tablespoon apple cider vinegar
- 1/2 Teaspoon ground cinnamon
- 1/8 Teaspoon ground cloves
- 2/3 ham

Directions:

1. Supply your smoker with wood pellets and follow the start-up procedure. Preheat the grill, with the lid closed, to 325° F.

2. Meanwhile, make the glaze: In a small saucepan, combine the orange juice, the maple syrup, marmalade, mustard, vinegar, cinnamon, and cloves.

3. Warm over low heat, whisking to combine the ingredients. Remove from the heat and reserve.

4. Place ham in large roasting pan lined with aluminum foil. Place pan on grill and cook for 1.5 hours. Grill: 325 °F

5. Open grill and glaze ham with reserved mixture. Continue cooking for another 30 minutes or until a thermometer is inserted into the thickest part of the meat and reaches an internal temperatures of 135 degrees F. Grill: 325 °F Probe: 135 °F

6. Remove ham from grill and allow to rest for 20 minutes before serving.

7. Warm remaining sauce and serve with ham if desired. Enjoy!

Hawaiian Pulled Pork

Servings: 8-10
Cooking Time: 640 Minutes

Ingredients:

- 2 Cups Aloe Leaf Juice
- 1 Tsp Coriander, Ground
- 2 Tsp Cracked Pepper
- 1 Tsp Cumin
- Dash Of Salt
- 4-6 Garlic, Cloves
- 1 (3-Inch) Ginger, Fresh
- 1-2 Limes
- 4 Cups No Sodium Added Chicken Bone Broth
- ¼ Cup Olive Oil
- 4 Tsp Paprika
- 6-8 Lbs Pork Shoulder/Butt
- 1/2 Sweet Onion
- 2 Packets Truvia To Sweeten Above Aloe Juice
- 2 Tbs Or 2 Tbs Swerve Brown Sugar Truvia – Honey Substitute

Directions:

1. Supply your smoker with wood pellets and follow the start-up procedure. Preheat the grill, with the lid closed, to 300° F. Make sure your flame broiler is closed, you want to use indirect heat for this recipe.

2. Add all spices into a bowl (salt, paprika, cumin, coriander, pepper, onion powder if needed). Set bowl aside.

3. Grate the ginger into a separate bowl (wet ingredients bowl).

4. Mince or smash the garlic cloves into the same bowl.

5. Dice onion and add it to the ginger and garlic (if no onion sub onion powder).

6. Juice 1-2 limes and add to the "wet" ingredients bowl.

7. Add 4 cups chicken bone broth.

8. Add two cups aloe leaf juice w/lemon and add two packets Truvia to sweeten.

9. Add 1-2 tbsp Truvia honey substitute. Mix and set bowl aside.

10. Add the oil to your Cast Iron and coat the bottom and sides. Place the pork in the cast iron roasting pan.

11. Take your dry rub and coat the pork.

12. Pour the wet ingredients around the pork, into the Cast Iron Roasting Pan.

13. Cover the roasting pan with the lid and set it on your grill.

14. Check the pork every couple hours (basting if you prefer). When internal temperature reaches 195°F (after around 6 – 8 hours of cook time), it should easily start to pull apart. Don't pull apart the whole shoulder yet.

15. Remove the Roasting Pan from the grill and set aside to allow it to rest for 1 hour. Remove the lid to help speed cooling.

16. Once cooled, shred the pork into a separate bowl, removing the fat as you go.

17. If you want to add some of the marinade to the pork for additional flavor, make sure you skim the fat off the top first and discard.

18. Viola! Pair with fresh grilled veggies, delicious fruit or make tacos or salads! So many options for this type of protein.

First-timer's Pulled Pork

Servings: 8
Cooking Time: 540 Minutes

Ingredients:
- 1 bone-in pork shoulder, about 5 to 7lb (2.3 to 3.2kg)
- coarse salt
- freshly ground black pepper
- 1½ cups low-carb beer or sugar-free dark-colored soda
- for the sauce
- 1½ cups apple cider vinegar
- ½ cup distilled water
- 2 tbsp ketchup
- 1½ tbsp granulated brown sugar or low-carb substitute
- 1 tsp coarse salt, plus more
- 1 tsp freshly ground black pepper
- ½ to 1 tsp crushed red pepper flakes

Directions:
1. Supply your smoker with wood pellets and follow the start-up procedure. Preheat the grill, with the lid closed, to 250° F.

2. In a medium saucepan on the stovetop over medium-high, make the vinegar sauce by bringing the ingredients to a boil. Whisk to dissolve the sugar and salt. Let the sauce cool to room temperature and then transfer to a jar with a tight-fitting lid. Set aside.

3. Season the pork shoulder on all sides with salt and pepper. Place the pork on the grate and smoke until the bone releases easily from the meat and the internal temperature reaches 200°F (93°C), about 7 to 9 hours. Wrap the pork tightly in a large piece of heavy-duty aluminum foil and let rest in an insulated cooler for up to 1 hour.

4. Carefully remove the pork from the foil and reserve the juices. Wear heatproof gloves to pull the pork into chunks. Discard the bone and any large lumps of fat. Pull the meat into shreds and transfer to a clean aluminum foil roasting pan. Moisten with some of the reserved juices. Taste, adding more salt and pepper. Serve with the vinegar sauce.

Baked German Pork Schnitzel With Grilled Lemons

Servings: 2

Cooking Time: 20 Minutes

Ingredients:

- 16 Ounce pork chops
- salt
- black pepper
- 1 Teaspoon garlic powder
- 1 Teaspoon paprika
- 2 eggs
- 1 Cup panko breadcrumbs
- 1/2 Cup flour
- 2 Whole lemon, halved

Directions:

1. Supply your smoker with wood pellets and follow the start-up procedure. Preheat the grill, with the lid closed, to High heat.

2. Place pork chops individually between 2 pieces of plastic wrap. Pound with a meat mallet until they are around 1/4 to 1/8" thick. Season both sides generously with salt and black pepper.

3. Mix the garlic powder and paprika in a bowl. In another bowl whisk the eggs. In a third bowl add the breadcrumbs.

4. Dip pork cutlets one by one into flour shaking off any excess, then into eggs and then into the breadcrumbs. Place breaded pork cutlets onto a lightly oiled wire rack over a baking sheet.

5. Cook for 15 minutes then flip and bake for another 5 minutes. When you open the grill to flip pork, place sliced lemons directly on grill grate flesh side down. Grill: 500 °F

6. Remove from grill and serve immediately with grilled lemons. Enjoy!

Asian-style Pork Tenderloin

Servings: 6

Cooking Time: 15 Minutes

Ingredients:

- 2 Whole Pork Tenderloin, 8-10 oz each
- 2 Tablespoon canola oil
- 2 Tablespoon Sambai Oelek
- 1 Teaspoon sesame oil
- 1 Teaspoon garlic, minced
- 1 Teaspoon fresh ginger
- 1 Teaspoon fish sauce
- 1 Teaspoon soy sauce
- 1/4 Cup brown sugar

Directions:

1. Use a sharp paring knife to remove the silver skin of the pork tenderloin.

2. Combine all the ingredients together. Cover the tenderloins in the mixture and allow them to marinate in the refrigerator for 30 minutes.

3. Supply your smoker with wood pellets and follow the start-up procedure. Preheat the grill, with the lid closed, to 450° F.

4. Place the loins towards the very front of the grill; turn periodically until there are dark grill marks all around. Transfer them to the middle of the grill to finish cooking. Cook for an addition 7-10 minutes for a medium rare tenderloin. When they are done cooking, remove them from the grill and let them rest for 10 minutes before slicing. Enjoy!

Delicious Pulled Pork Poutine

Servings: 4
Cooking Time: 240 Minutes

Ingredients:

- 2 Tbsp Apple Cider Vinegar
- 1/2 Cup Bbq Sauce
- 1 1/2 Cups Beef Stock
- 2 Tbsp Butter
- For Assembly, Cheese Curds
- 2 Cups Chicken Stock
- 2 Tbsp Flour
- For Assembly, French Fries
- 3 Garlic Cloves, Minced
- 1 Tbsp Olive Oil
- 2 1/2 Lbs Pork Shoulder Roast, Bone-In
- To Taste, Pulled Pork Rub
- For Assembly, Sliced Scallions
- 1/2 Yellow Onion, Minced
- 1/2 Yellow Onion, Sliced

Directions:

1. Supply your smoker with wood pellets and follow the start-up procedure. Preheat the grill, with the lid open, to 225° F. If using a gas or charcoal grill, set it up for low, indirect heat.
2. Season the pork shoulder with a pork rub, then transfer to the grill grate, fat side up. Smoke the pork shoulder for 2 ½ hours.
3. Add chicken stock, vinegar, and sliced onion to a Dutch oven. Transfer the smoked pork shoulder to the Dutch oven, then cover and increase the grill temperature to 325° F. Braise the pork shoulder for 1 ½ hours, until tender.
4. When tender, remove the pork from the grill and rest for 20 minutes, then shred.
5. While the pork is resting, prepare the gravy: set a cast iron skillet on the grill. Heat the butter and olive oil in the skillet, then sauté the onion and garlic for 2 minutes, stirring often. Stir in the flour and cook for 1 minute. Slowly add the beef stock, and stir until thickened. Add bbq sauce and simmer for 3 minutes. Remove from the grill and set aside for assembly.
6. Assemble the poutine: spread out a layer of French fries, then layer gravy, pulled pork, cheese curds, additional gravy, and scallions. Serve warm.

Baked Maple And Brown Sugar Bacon

Servings: 4
Cooking Time: 60 Minutes

Ingredients:

- 1 Pound cold bacon
- 1/2 Cup pure maple syrup, warmed
- 1/2 Cup brown sugar, plus more as needed

Directions:

1. Supply your smoker with wood pellets and follow the start-up procedure. Preheat the grill, with the lid closed, to 300° F.
2. Line a rimmed baking sheet with foil and place a wire rack on top. Lay bacon strips in a single layer on the wire rack.
3. Using a pastry brush, brush each strip of bacon on both sides with the warmed maple syrup, then sprinkle brown sugar evenly on both sides.
4. Put the baking sheet in the grill and cook bacon for 60-75 minutes, or until bacon browns and appears to be crisping. Grill: 300 ℉
5. Allow the bacon to cool slightly before eating. Enjoy!

Pork Tenderloin With Bourbon Peaches

Servings: 6
Cooking Time: 27 Minutes

Ingredients:

- 2 pork tenderloins, about 2lb (1kg) total, trimmed of silver skin and excess fat
- extra virgin olive oil
- for the rub
- 3 tbsp coarse salt
- 3 tbsp freshly ground black pepper
- 3 tbsp smoked or regular paprika
- 3 tbsp granulated light brown sugar or low-carb substitute
- 2 tbsp instant coffee
- 1 tbsp granulated garlic
- 2 tsp ground cumin
- 1 tsp chili powder
- for the peaches
- 4 freestone peaches, about 1lb (450g) total, peeled, pitted, and sliced
- 1 tbsp freshly squeezed lemon juice
- ¼ cup unsalted butter
- 4 tbsp granulated light brown sugar or low-carb substitute
- 2 tbsp bourbon
- ½ tsp ground cinnamon
- ½ tsp pure vanilla extract
- pinch of coarse salt

Directions:

1. Supply your smoker with wood pellets and follow the start-up procedure. Preheat the grill, with the lid closed, to 400° F.
2. In a small bowl, make the rub by combining the ingredients. Coat the tenderloins in olive oil and season with the rub.
3. Place the peaches and lemon juice in a medium bowl, turning the peaches gently to coat. Measure the other ingredients and then take them and the peaches grill side.
4. Place 1 tablespoon of olive oil in the hot skillet and add the tenderloins. Quickly sear the pork, about 2 to 3 minute per side, turning as needed with tongs. When they're nicely browned, transfer the tenderloins to the grate. Cook until the internal temperature in the thickest part of the meat reaches 145°F (63°C), about 8 minutes. For moist meat, don't cook the tenderloins beyond 155°F (68°C).
5. Transfer the pork to a cutting board and tent with aluminum foil.
6. Replace the cast iron skillet with a clean one and close the grill lid to let it heat. Once hot, make the bourbon peaches by melting the butter. Add the brown sugar, bourbon, cinnamon, vanilla, and salt. Cook the mixture until it bubbles, about 5 to 8 minutes. Add the peaches and cook for 5 to 8 minutes more, turning the peaches carefully with a spoon to coat. Carefully transfer the skillet to a trivet or another heatproof surface.
7. Slice the pork on a diagonal into ½-inch (1.25cm) slices. Shingle the slices on a platter. Spoon the peaches around the pork or serve separately.

Baked Candied Bacon Cinnamon Rolls

Servings: 6
Cooking Time: 35 Minutes

Ingredients:

- 12 Slices Bacon, sliced
- 1/3 Cup brown sugar
- pre-made cinnamon rolls

- 2 Ounce cream cheese

Directions:

1. Supply your smoker with wood pellets and follow the start-up procedure. Preheat the grill, with the lid closed, to 350° F.

2. Dredge 8 of the slices of bacon in brown sugar, making sure to cover both sides of the bacon.

3. Place the brown sugared bacon slices along with the other slices of bacon on a cooling rack placed on top of a large baking sheet.

4. Cook the bacon on the Traeger for 15-20 minutes or until the fat renders but bacon is still pliable. Turn the Traeger down to 325°F.

5. Open and unroll the cinnamon rolls. While bacon is still warm, place 1 slice of the brown sugared bacon on top of 1 of the unrolled rolls and roll back up. Repeat for all the rolls.

6. Place cinnamon rolls in an 8" x 8" baking dish or cake pan that has been sprayed with nonstick cooking spray. Cook the cinnamon rolls at 325°F for 10 to 15 minutes or until golden. Rotate the pan a half turn halfway through cooking time. Grill: 325 °F

7. Meanwhile, take the provided cream cheese frosting and mix in the softened cream cheese. Crumble the cooked bacon and add into the cream cheese frosting.

8. Spread frosting over warm cinnamon rolls. Serve warm, enjoy!

Baked Beans

Servings: 12
Cooking Time: 180 Minutes

Ingredients:
- 1 Pack Bacon
- 1/2 Cup Brown Sugar
- 1 Coca Cola, Can
- 2 Cans Mixed Beans
- 1/3 Cup Molasses
- 4 Cans Pork And Beans
- 1 Red Onion, Chopped
- 1/3 Cup Yellow Mustard

Directions:

1. Supply your smoker with wood pellets and follow the start-up procedure. Preheat the grill, with the lid closed, to 275° F.

2. Combine all the ingredients and stir until combined.

3. Smoked for 2.5 hours covered. For the last 30 minutes, smoke uncovered.

4. Serve hot. Enjoy!

Grilled Raspberry Chipotle Pork Ribs

Servings: 4
Cooking Time: 180 Minutes

Ingredients:
- Baby Back Rib
- Original Bbq Sauce
- Raspberry Chipotle Spice Rub

Directions:

1. Begin by gently rinsing off your ribs in cool water. Pat dry and remove the flavor blocker (thin membrane on the underside of the ribs) to allow the seasoning to permeate right into the meat.

2. Generously season your ribs with Raspberry Chipotle seasoning and place in the refrigerator for an hour for flavor to set in.

3. Supply your smoker with wood pellets and follow the start-up procedure. Preheat the grill, with the lid open, to 250° F. Place your seasoned rack of ribs on the grill and let cook for 2 hours.

Next, lather on a thick coating of Original BBQ Sauce, turn up the grill to 300°F and let your ribs roast for another hour. Remove, cut and serve for a meal that will surely make its way into the weekly rotation.

Smoked Bbq Ribs

Servings: 4

Cooking Time: 300 Minutes

Ingredients:
- 2 Rack St. Louis-style ribs
- 1/4 Cup Big Game Rub
- 1 Cup apple juice
- BBQ Sauce

Directions:

1. Pat ribs dry and peel the membrane from the back of the ribs.

2. Apply an even coat of rub to the front, back and sides of the ribs. Let sit for 20 minutes and up to 4 hours if refrigerated.

3. Supply your smoker with wood pellets and follow the start-up procedure. Preheat the grill, with the lid closed, to 225° F.

4. Place ribs, bone side down on grill. Put apple juice in a spray bottle and spray the ribs after 1 hour of cooking. Spray every 45 minutes thereafter. Grill: 225 °F Probe: 201 °F

5. After 4-1/2 hours, check the internal temperature of ribs. Ribs are done when internal temperature reaches 201°F. If not, check back in another 30 minutes. Grill: 225 °F Probe: 201 °F

6. Once ribs are done, brush a light layer of your favorite Traeger BBQ Sauce on the front and back of the ribs. Let the sauce set for 10 minutes. After the sauce has set, take ribs off the grill and let rest for 10 minutes. Slice ribs in between the bones and serve with extra sauce. Enjoy!

VEGETABLES RECIPES

Grilled Asparagus And Spinach Salad

Servings: 8
Cooking Time: 10 Minutes

Ingredients:
- 4 Fluid Ounce apple cider vinegar
- 8 Fluid Ounce Honey Bourbon BBQ Sauce
- 2 Bunch asparagus, ends trimmed
- 3 Fluid Ounce extra-virgin olive oil
- 2 Ounce Beef Rub
- 24 Ounce Spinach, fresh
- 4 Ounce candied pecans
- 4 Ounce feta cheese

Directions:
1. Combine apple cider vinegar and Traeger Apricot BBQ Sauce to create salad dressing.
2. Supply your smoker with wood pellets and follow the start-up procedure. Preheat the grill, with the lid closed, to High heat.
3. Toss the asparagus with Olive Oil and the Beef Shake. Put asparagus in the Traeger Grilling Basket and move the basket to the grill grate.
4. Grill for about 10 minutes. Remove the asparagus once it is cooked. Grill: 350 °F
5. Place the hot asparagus right on top of the bowl of spinach.
6. Add candied pecans, feta cheese & salad dressing then toss and serve. Enjoy!

Sicilian Stuffed Mushrooms

Servings: 6
Cooking Time: 25 Minutes

Ingredients:

- 12 Medium Fresh Mushrooms, about 1-1/2 inches in diameter
- 4 Ounce cream cheese, room temperature
- 1/4 Cup Parmesan cheese, grated
- 1/4 Cup shredded mozzarella cheese
- 8 Whole Pimento Stuffed Green Olives, chopped
- 3 Tablespoon Pepperoni, finely diced
- 1 1/2 Tablespoon Sun Dried Tomatoes, drained & minced
- 1/4 Teaspoon freshly ground black pepper

Directions:
1. Dampen a paper towel and wipe the outside of the mushrooms clean. Remove the stem. Using a small spoon, scoop out the inside of the mushroom leaving a shell.
2. Filling: In a small mixing bowl, beat together the cream cheese, Parmesan, and mozzarella. Stir in olives, pepperoni, tomatoes, basil, and pepper.
3. Mound the filling in the mushroom caps. Set each filled cap into the well of a muffin tin.
4. Supply your smoker with wood pellets and follow the start-up procedure. Preheat the grill, with the lid closed, to 350° F.
5. Arrange the muffin tin on the grill grate and bake the mushrooms for 25 to 30 minutes, or until the mushrooms are tender and the filling is beginning to brown.
6. Transfer to a serving plate or platter. Enjoy!

Tater Tot Bake

Servings: 4
Cooking Time: 15 Minutes

Ingredients:
- 1 Whole frozen tater tots

- salt and pepper
- 1 Cup sour cream
- 1 Cup shredded cheddar cheese, divided
- 1/2 Cup bacon, chopped
- 1/4 Cup green onion, diced

Directions:

1. Supply your smoker with wood pellets and follow the start-up procedure. Preheat the grill, with the lid closed, to 375° F.

2. Line a baking sheet with aluminum foil for easy clean up and spread frozen tater tots onto sheet.

3. Sprinkle with Veggie Shake or salt and pepper to taste.

4. Place the baking sheet on the preheated grill grate and cook the tater tots for 10 minutes.

5. Drizzle sour cream over cooked tater tots.

6. Sprinkle the cheese, bacon bits and green onions on top of the tater tots.

7. Turn heat up to High heat and cook for 5 more minutes until the cheese melts and serve immediately. Enjoy!

Skillet Potato Cake

Servings: 4

Cooking Time: 40 Minutes

Ingredients:

- 8 Tablespoon butter, melted
- 2 Pound russet potatoes, peeled and thinly sliced
- 3 Tablespoon kosher salt
- 2 Tablespoon freshly ground black pepper
- thyme

Directions:

1. Supply your smoker with wood pellets and follow the start-up procedure. Preheat the grill, with the lid closed, to 375° F.

2. Brush the bottom of a cast iron skillet with part of the melted butter. Place potato slices vertically around the outer edges then fill in the middle in the same fashion.

3. Pour additional melted butter over the top of the layers and sprinkle with salt and pepper.

4. Place skillet in grill and cook for 35 to 40 minutes or until potatoes are fork tender and golden brown.

5. Garnish with a sprinkle of fresh thyme over the top of the potatoes. Enjoy!

Smoked Mushrooms

Servings: 4

Cooking Time: 45 Minutes

Ingredients:

- Pound Mushrooms, fresh
- 1/2 Cup apple cider vinegar
- 1/2 Cup soy sauce
- 1 Teaspoon Blackened Saskatchewan Rub

Directions:

1. Clean mushrooms and place in a large Ziploc bag. Add apple cider vinegar, soy sauce and rub.

2. Mix well and allow to marinate in the refrigerator for at least 2 hours.

3. Supply your smoker with wood pellets and follow the start-up procedure. Preheat the grill, with the lid closed, to 350° F.

4. Place cast iron skillet inside grill for 20 minutes to warm up.

5. Add the mushrooms and marinade slowly into the cast iron skillet.

6. Cook uncovered for 15 minutes, then cover the skillet and cook another 30 minutes until mushrooms are tender. Grill: 350 °F

7. Remove skillet from grill and let mushrooms cool down for 5 minutes before serving. Enjoy!

Traeger Smoked Coleslaw

Servings: 8
Cooking Time: 20 Minutes

Ingredients:
- 1 Head purple cabbage, shredded
- 1 Head green cabbage, shredded
- 1 Cup shredded carrots
- 2 scallions, thinly sliced
- 1 1/2 Cup mayonnaise
- 1/8 Cup white wine vinegar
- 1 Teaspoon celery seed
- 1 Teaspoon sugar
- salt and pepper

Directions:
1. Supply your smoker with wood pellets and follow the start-up procedure. Preheat the grill, with the lid closed, to 180° F.
2. Spread cabbage and carrots out on a sheet tray and place directly on the grill grates. Smoke for 20 to 25 minutes or until cabbage picks up desired amount of smoke. Grill: 180 °F
3. Remove from grill and transfer to the refrigerator immediately to cool. While cabbage is cooling, make the dressing.
4. For the dressing, combine all ingredients in a small bowl and mix well.
5. Place smoked cabbage and carrots in a large bowl and pour dressing over them. Stir to coat well.
6. Transfer to a serving dish and sprinkle with scallions. Enjoy!

Baked Stuffed Avocados

Servings: 6
Cooking Time: 15 Minutes

Ingredients:
- 4 avocados, halved and pit removed
- 8 eggs
- 2 Cup shredded cheddar cheese
- 1/4 Cup cherry tomatoes, halved
- 4 Slices Bacon, cooked & chopped
- salt and pepper
- 1 scallion, thinly sliced

Directions:
1. Supply your smoker with wood pellets and follow the start-up procedure. Preheat the grill, with the lid closed, to 450° F.
2. After removing the pit from the avocado, scoop out a little of the flesh to make enough room to fit 1 egg per half.
3. Fill the bottom of a cast iron pan with kosher salt and nestle the avocado halves into the salt, cut side up. The salt helps to keep them in place while cooking, like ice with oysters.
4. Crack one egg into each half, top with shredded cheddar cheese, cherry tomatoes and bacon. Season with salt and pepper to taste.
5. Place the cast iron pan directly on the grill grate and bake the avocados for 12 to 15 minutes until the cheese is melted and the egg is just set. Grill: 450 °F
6. Remove from the grill and let rest 5 to 10 minutes. Top with sliced scallions and enjoy!

Grilled Ratatouille Salad

Servings: 4
Cooking Time: 25 Minutes

Ingredients:
- 1 Whole sweet potatoes
- 1 Whole red onion, diced
- 1 Whole zucchini
- 1 Whole Squash
- 1 Large Tomato, diced

- vegetable oil
- salt and pepper

Directions:

1. Supply your smoker with wood pellets and follow the start-up procedure. Preheat the grill, with the lid closed, to High heat.

2. Slice all vegetables to a ¼ inch thickness.

3. Lightly brush each vegetable with oil and season with Traeger's Veggie Shake or salt and pepper.

4. Place sweet potato, onion, zucchini, and squash on grill grate and grill for 20 minutes or until tender, turn halfway through.

5. Add tomato slices to the grill during the last 5 minutes of cooking time.

6. For presentation, alternate vegetables while layering them vertically. Enjoy!

Red Potato Grilled Lollipops

Servings: 4

Cooking Time: 25 Minutes

Ingredients:

- 8 Large red bliss potatoes, halved
- 2 Clove garlic, minced
- 2 Sprig rosemary, minced
- 2 Tablespoon olive oil
- 1 Teaspoon salt
- 1/2 Teaspoon black pepper
- 5 Wooden Skewers, soaked in water
- 1/4 Cup Parmesan cheese, grated

Directions:

1. Supply your smoker with wood pellets and follow the start-up procedure. Preheat the grill, with the lid closed, to 450° F.

2. Halve potatoes and poke each several times with a fork.

3. Put the potatoes in a large bowl and toss with the minced garlic, rosemary leaves, a few tablespoons of olive oil, kosher salt, and pepper. Microwave the potatoes for 4 minutes. Gently toss potatoes and microwave for another 3 minutes.

4. Skewer potato halves threading about 4 or 5 potato halves on each skewer. Brush potatoes with olive oil.

5. Place the potato skewers on the Traeger, cut side down, and grill until the sides begin to brown (4-7 minutes).

6. Flip and grill skin side down for another 7-10 minutes.

7. They are done when a sharp knife tip easily penetrates the sides. Remove potatoes from grill and top with grated parmesan cheese. Enjoy!

Whole Roasted Cauliflower With Garlic Parmesan Butter

Servings: 4

Cooking Time: 45 Minutes

Ingredients:

- 1 Whole head cauliflower
- 1/4 Cup olive oil
- salt and pepper
- 1/2 Cup butter, melted
- 1/4 Cup shredded Parmesan cheese
- 2 Clove garlic, minced
- 1/2 Tablespoon chopped parsley

Directions:

1. Supply your smoker with wood pellets and follow the start-up procedure. Preheat the grill, with the lid closed, to 450° F.

2. Brush the cauliflower with olive oil and season liberally with salt and pepper.

3. Put cauliflower in a cast iron skillet, place directly on the grill grate and cook for 45 minutes until golden brown and the center is tender.

4. While the cauliflower is cooking, combine the melted butter, parmesan, garlic and parsley in a small bowl.

5. During the last 20 minutes of cooking, baste the cauliflower with the melted butter mixture.

6. Remove the cauliflower from the grill and top with extra parmesan and parsley if desired. Enjoy!

Roasted Potato Poutine

Servings: 6
Cooking Time: 40 Minutes

Ingredients:

- 4 Large russet potatoes
- Tablespoon olive oil or vegetable oil
- Prime Rib Rub
- Cup chicken or beef gravy (homemade or jarred)
- 1 1/2 Cup white or yellow cheddar cheese curds
- freshly ground black pepper
- 2 Tablespoon scallions

Directions:

1. Supply your smoker with wood pellets and follow the start-up procedure. Preheat the grill, with the lid closed, to 500° F.

2. Scrub the potatoes and slice into fries, wedges or preferred shape.

3. Put potatoes into a large mixing bowl and coat with oil. Season generously with Traeger Prime Rib rub.

4. Tip the potatoes onto a rimmed baking sheet and spread in a single layer, cut sides down.

5. Roast for 20 minutes, then using a spatula, turn the potatoes to the other cut side. Continue to roast until the potatoes are tender and golden brown, about 15 to 20 minutes more.

6. While potatoes cook, warm the gravy on the stovetop or in a heat-proof saucepan on your Traeger.

7. To assemble the poutine, arrange the potatoes in a large shallow bowl or on a serving platter. Distribute the cheese curds on top. Pour the hot gravy evenly over the potatoes and cheese curds.

8. Season with black pepper and garnish with thinly sliced scallions. Serve immediately. Enjoy!

Baked Sweet And Savory Yams By Bennie Kendrick

Servings: 6
Cooking Time: 60 Minutes

Ingredients:

- 3 Medium Yams
- 3 Tablespoon extra-virgin olive oil
- honey
- Goat Cheese
- 1/2 Cup brown sugar
- 1/2 Cup Pecans, pieces

Directions:

1. Supply your smoker with wood pellets and follow the start-up procedure. Preheat the grill, with the lid closed, to 350° F.

2. While Traeger comes to temperature, wash yams and poke a few holes all over. Wrap yams in foil.

3. Bake for 45-60 minutes or until knife tender. You don't want to overcook and get the yams too soft because you want to be able to cut each yam into rounds.

4. Once yams have cooled to the touch, cut each into 1/4" rounds. Lightly coat each round with oil olive and place on sheet tray.

5. Sprinkle each top with brown sugar. Using a teaspoon, place desired amount of goat cheese on each round. Next top with chopped pecans. Finally, drizzle Bee Local honey over each round.

6. Based on how sweet you like your yams, you can add more brown sugar and honey.

7. After complete, place your sheet tray back in the grill and cook, lid closed, for another 20 minutes. Enjoy!

Roasted Pumpkin Seeds

Servings: 8
Cooking Time: 40 Minutes

Ingredients:
- 1 Whole Pumpkin, seeds
- olive oil or vegetable oil
- Jacobsen Salt Co. Pure Kosher Sea Salt

Directions:
1. As soon as possible after removing the seeds from the pumpkin, rinse pumpkin seeds under cold water in a colander and pick out the pulp and strings.

2. Place the pumpkin seeds in a single layer on an oiled baking sheet, stirring to coat. Supply your smoker with wood pellets and follow the start-up procedure. Preheat the grill, with the lid closed, to 180° F.

3. Place the baking sheet with the seeds on the grill grate, close the lid, and smoke for 20 minutes. Grill: 180 °F

4. Sprinkle your seeds with salt and turn the temperature on your grill up to 325°F. Roast the seeds until toasted, about 20 minutes. Check and stir seeds after the first 10 minutes. Grill: 325 °F

5. Seeds will be brown because they were smoked before being roasted. Enjoy!

Blt Pasta Salad

Servings: 6
Cooking Time: 45 Minutes

Ingredients:
- 1 pound thick-cut bacon
- 16 ounces bowtie pasta, cooked according to package directions and drained
- 2 tomatoes, chopped
- ½ cup chopped scallions
- ½ cup Italian dressing
- ½ cup ranch dressing
- 1 tablespoon chopped fresh basil
- 1 teaspoon salt
- 1 teaspoon freshly ground black pepper
- 1 teaspoon garlic powder
- 1 head lettuce, cored and torn

Directions:
1. Supply your smoker with wood pellets and follow the start-up procedure. Preheat, with the lid closed, to 225°F.

2. Arrange the bacon slices on the grill grate, close the lid, and cook for 30 to 45 minutes, flipping after 20 minutes, until crisp.

3. Remove the bacon from the grill and chop.

4. In a large bowl, combine the chopped bacon with the cooked pasta, tomatoes, scallions, Italian dressing, ranch dressing, basil, salt, pepper, and garlic powder. Refrigerate until ready to serve.

5. Toss in the lettuce just before serving to keep it from wilting.

Grilled Fingerling Potato Salad

Servings: 6
Cooking Time: 15 Minutes

Ingredients:
* 10 Whole scallions
* 2/3 Cup extra-virgin olive oil, divided
* 1 1/2 Pound fingerling potatoes, cut in half lengthwise
* pepper
* 2 Teaspoon kosher salt, divided, plus more as needed
* 2 Tablespoon rice vinegar
* 2 Teaspoon lemon juice
* 1 Small jalapeño, sliced

Directions:
1. Supply your smoker with wood pellets and follow the start-up procedure. Preheat the grill, with the lid closed, to 450° F.
2. Brush the scallions with oil and place on the grill.
3. Cook until lightly charred, about 2 to 3 minutes. Remove and let cool. Grill: 450 °F
4. Once the scallions have cooled, slice and set aside.
5. Brush the fingerling potatoes with oil (reserving 1/3 cup for later use), then salt and pepper. Place cut-side down on the grill until cooked through, about 4 to 5 minutes. Grill: 450 °F
6. In a bowl, whisk the remaining 1/3 cup olive oil, 1 teaspoon salt, rice vinegar and lemon juice. Next mix in the scallions, potatoes and sliced jalapeño.
7. Season with salt and pepper, and serve. Enjoy!

Traeger Grilled Whole Corn

Servings: 4

Cooking Time: 25 Minutes

Ingredients:
* 3 green onions
* 6 Tablespoon butter, softened
* 1 Teaspoon chile powder
* 1 Teaspoon toasted sesame seeds
* 4 ears corn, in husk

Directions:
1. Supply your smoker with wood pellets and follow the start-up procedure. Preheat the grill, with the lid closed, to 325° F.
2. Place green onions directly on the grill grate and cook 15 minutes until lightly charred. Remove from grill and set aside.
3. Sesame-Chile Butter: Take butter out of fridge and let soften. Chop up charred green onions and add to butter along with chile powder and sesame seeds. Mash all ingredients together.
4. Grill corn, rotating occasionally, until husks are blackened (some will flake and fall off) and kernels are tender with some browned and charred spots, about 25 to 35 minutes. Grill: 325 °F
5. Let corn cool slightly, then shuck. Serve with the Sesame-Chile Butter. Enjoy

Braised Creamed Green Beans

Servings: 4
Cooking Time: 25 Minutes

Ingredients:
* 6 Tablespoon butter
* 2 Clove garlic, pressed or minced
* 1 shallot, thinly sliced
* 1 Cup heavy cream
* 1 Pinch ground nutmeg
* salt

- 3 Pound mixed greens such as kale, chard or collards; washed, stems removed and torn into bite sized pieces

Directions:

1. Supply your smoker with wood pellets and follow the start-up procedure. Preheat the grill, with the lid closed, to 325° F.

2. In a saucepan, heat 2 tablespoons of the butter over high heat until it foams. Add the garlic and shallot and cook over medium-low heat, stirring, until softened and golden, about 5 minutes.

3. Add the cream, bring to a simmer and cook until slightly thickened, about 10 minutes.

4. Add the nutmeg and salt to taste. Using a hand blender, purée until smooth.

5. In a cast iron pan, heat the remaining 4 tablespoons butter over high heat until it foams.

6. Add the greens and cook until tender but still bright green, about 5 minutes.

7. Sprinkle with salt and add the cream mixture. Cover and transfer to the grill.

8. Braise greens for 15-20 minutes until the cream is bubbling and greens are tender. Grill: 325 °F

9. Season to taste with nutmeg and salt. Serve hot. Enjoy!

Roasted Red Pepper White Bean Dip

Servings: 4
Cooking Time: 40 Minutes

Ingredients:
- 4 Whole garlic
- 4 Tablespoon extra-virgin olive oil
- 2 Bell Pepper, Red
- 3 Tablespoon Dill Weed, fresh
- 3 Tablespoon chopped flat-leaf parsley
- 2 Can cannellini beans, mashed
- 4 Teaspoon lemon juice
- 1 1/2 Teaspoon salt

Directions:

1. Roasting the garlic and red peppers:

2. Supply your smoker with wood pellets and follow the start-up procedure. Preheat the grill, with the lid closed, to 400° F.

3. Peel away the outside layers of the garlic husk. Cut off the top of the garlic bulb, exposing each of the individual cloves. Drizzle olive oil over the top of the head of garlic and rub it in. Wrap the garlic in foil, completely covering it. Put the head of garlic and the two red peppers (washed and dried) on the Traeger.

4. Roast the garlic for 25-30 minutes and the peppers for about 40 minutes. Rotate the peppers a quarter-turn every 10 minutes until the exterior is blistered and blackened. Grill: 400 °F

5. Pull the peppers off the grill and put them in a bowl. Cover the bowl with plastic wrap and leave them for 15 minutes. The steam will loosen the skins so that they slip off like a drumstick covered in barbecue sauce.

6. Peel off the pepper skin. Cut off the stems and scrape out the seeds and they're ready to use.

7. As for the garlic, let it cool and then pull out the individual cloves as needed.

8. The dip:

9. In a blender put the roasted red peppers, 4 cloves of roasted garlic, dill, parsley, drained and rinsed beans, olive oil, lemon juice and salt.

10. Blend until the dip is smooth and creamy. You may need to scrape down the sides of the blender a couple of times. If it's having difficulty blending or looks too thick add more olive oil or lemon juice. (Add more lemon juice if it tastes like it needs more acid or brightness.) Enjoy!

Roasted Do-ahead Mashed Potatoes

Servings: 6
Cooking Time: 50 Minutes

Ingredients:

* 5 Pound Yukon Gold or russet potatoes
* 9 Tablespoon butter
* 8 Ounce cream cheese
* 1/2 Cup milk
* salt and pepper

Directions:

1. Peel the potatoes and cut into chunks that are roughly the same size. Cover with cold water and add a teaspoon of salt. Bring to a boil over high heat, then reduce the heat to medium and simmer the potatoes until they are tender.
2. Drain the potatoes and return them to the pot. Stir over low heat for 2 to 3 minutes to evaporate any excess moisture.
3. Mash the potatoes with a hand-held potato masher. (Alternative, rice the potatoes using a ricer.) Incorporate 8 tbsp butter and cream cheese. Add milk until the potatoes are of a good consistency. Stir in salt and pepper to taste.
4. Butter the inside of a casserole dish. Spread the potatoes out in an even layer in the casserole dish, smoothing the top with a spatula. Cool, cover, and refrigerate if not cooking right away. Before cooking, let the potatoes warm to room temperature (about an hour).
5. Supply your smoker with wood pellets and follow the start-up procedure. Preheat the grill, with the lid closed, to 350° F.
6. Bake the potatoes for 45 to 50 minutes, or until hot through. Grill: 350 °F

Green Bean Casserole

Servings: 6
Cooking Time: 25 Minutes

Ingredients:

* 1/2 Stick butter
* 1 Small onion
* 1/2 Cup sliced button mushrooms
* 4 Can green beans, drained
* 2 Can cream of mushroom soup
* 1 Teaspoon Lawry's Seasoned Salt
* pepper
* 1 Can French's Original Crispy Fried Onions
* 1 Cup grated sharp cheddar cheese

Directions:

1. Supply your smoker with wood pellets and follow the start-up procedure. Preheat the grill, with the lid closed, to 375° F.
2. Melt butter in a cast iron skillet and add onions and mushrooms, stirring occasionally until softened.
3. Add drained green beans and cream of mushroom soup and stir gently to combine.
4. Season with seasoned salt and pepper and sprinkle the top with grated cheddar cheese and fried onions.
5. Bake for 25 minutes. Serve warm, enjoy! Grill: 375 °F

Smoked Mashed Potatoes

Servings: 6
Cooking Time: 45 Minutes

Ingredients:

* 2 Pound red bliss potatoes, washed and diced medium
* chicken stock or water
* 1/2 Stick salted butter

- 1 Cup whole milk
- 1/2 Cup sour cream
- 1/2 Cup shredded or grated Parmesan cheese
- kosher salt
- freshly ground black pepper
- 1/2 Cup fresh sliced green onions

Directions:

1. Place the diced red potatoes into a small saucepan or stockpot and cover with chicken stock or water.

2. Bring to a boil and cook on a simmer until fork tender, then cook 4 to 5 minutes past that until soft.

3. Supply your smoker with wood pellets and follow the start-up procedure. Preheat the grill, with the lid closed, to 400° F.

4. In a separate ovenproof pan, such as a cast iron skillet, add butter and milk and place in the Traeger during start up, until melted (approximately 7 to 10 minutes). Grill: 400 °F

5. Carefully remove the butter/milk mixture from the Traeger using heatproof gloves.

6. Drain the potatoes and place into a large bowl. Add the melted butter/milk mixture and slowly mash.

7. Add sour cream, cheese and green onions, then season to taste with salt and pepper.

8. Place into the cast iron skillet, then place the skillet back into the Traeger and cook until the potatoes have a slight crust and are bubbling, about 15 minutes. Grill: 400 °F

9. Carefully remove the mashed potatoes from the Traeger using heatproof gloves. Allow to cool for 5 minutes. Scoop and enjoy!

Smoked Jalapeño Poppers

Servings: 4

Cooking Time: 60 Minutes

Ingredients:

- 12 Medium jalapeño
- 6 Slices bacon, cut in half
- 8 Ounce cream cheese
- 2 Tablespoon Pork & Poultry Rub
- 1 Cup grated cheese

Directions:

1. Supply your smoker with wood pellets and follow the start-up procedure. Preheat the grill, with the lid closed, to 180° F. For optimal flavor, use Super Smoke if available.

2. Slice the jalapeños in half lengthwise. Scrape out any seeds and ribs with a small spoon or paring knife. Mix softened cream cheese with Traeger Pork & Poultry rub and grated cheese. Spoon mixture onto each jalapeño half. Wrap with bacon and secure with a toothpick.

3. Place the jalapeños on a rimmed baking sheet. Place on grill and smoke for 30 minutes. Grill: 180 °F

4. Increase the grill temperature to 375°F and cook an additional 30 minutes or until bacon is cooked to desired doneness. Serve warm, enjoy! Grill: 375 °F

Baked Winter Squash Au Gratin

Servings: 8

Cooking Time: 45 Minutes

Ingredients:

- 2 Cup heavy cream
- salt and pepper
- 3 Cup shredded Gruyere cheese
- 4 Clove garlic, diced
- 2 Tablespoon butter
- 3 yellow potatoes, peeled and cubed
- 1 butternut squash seeded, peeled and cubed

- 1 acorn squash seeded, peeled and cubed

Directions:

1. Supply your smoker with wood pellets and follow the start-up procedure. Preheat the grill, with the lid closed, to 375° F.

2. In a medium saucepan, cook the cream, stirring constantly, until it comes to a low boil. Add salt, pepper, garlic and shredded Gruyere cheese. Stir until cheese is melted.

3. Grease a 9x13 inch baking dish with 2 tablespoons of butter. In a large mixing bowl, combine potatoes, butternut and acorn squash. Stir in the cheese sauce. Place mixture in the prepared baking dish and place in grill.

4. Cook for 45 minutes or until potatoes and squash are fork tender. Remove from grill and let cool for 10 minutes before serving. Enjoy! Grill: 375 °F

Smoked Pickled Green Beans

Servings: 4

Cooking Time: 45 Minutes

Ingredients:

- 1 Pound Green Beans, blanched
- 1/2 Cup salt
- 1/2 Cup sugar
- 1 Tablespoon red pepper flakes
- 2 Cup white wine vinegar
- 2 Cup ice water

Directions:

1. Supply your smoker with wood pellets and follow the start-up procedure. Preheat the grill, with the lid closed, to 180° F.

2. Place the blanched green beans on a mesh grill mat and place mat directly on the grill grate. Smoke the green beans for 30-45 minutes until they've picked up the desired amount of smoke.

Remove from grill and set aside until the brine is ready. Grill: 180 °F

3. In a medium sized saucepan, bring all remaining ingredients, except ice water, to a boil over medium high heat on the stove. Simmer for 5-10 minutes then remove from heat and steep 20 minutes more. Pour brine over ice water to cool.

4. Once brine has cooled, pour over the green beans and weigh them down with a few plates to ensure they are completely submerged. Let sit 24 hours before use. Enjoy!

Roasted Olives

Servings: 4

Cooking Time: 45 Minutes

Ingredients:

- 2 Cup mixed olives
- 3 Sprig fresh rosemary
- 2 Clove garlic, minced
- 2 Tablespoon orange zest
- 1/3 Cup extra-virgin olive oil
- 2 Tablespoon orange juice
- 1/2 Teaspoon red pepper flakes

Directions:

1. Combine the olives, rosemary, garlic, orange zest, red pepper flakes, olive oil, and orange juice in a glass oven-safe pie plate or baking dish. Cover with foil.

2. Supply your smoker with wood pellets and follow the start-up procedure. Preheat the grill, with the lid closed, to 300° F.

3. Roast the olives for 45 minutes, stirring once or twice. Serve warm in an attractive bowl. Enjoy! Grill: 300 °F

Roasted New Potatoes With Compound Butter

Servings: 4
Cooking Time: 45 Minutes

Ingredients:

- 2 Pound Small Red, White or Purple Potatoes (or Combination of All Three)
- 3 Tablespoon olive oil
- salt and pepper
- 2 Stick Butter, unsalted
- 1 Tablespoon shallot, minced
- 3 Tablespoon Finely Chopped Herbs, Such As Tarragon, Parsley, Basil or Combination
- 2 Teaspoon kosher salt

Directions:

1. Supply your smoker with wood pellets and follow the start-up procedure. Preheat the grill, with the lid closed, to 400° F. Cut the potatoes in half and place in a large mixing bowl. Cover with the olive oil, a teaspoon of salt and generous grinding of pepper.

2. Place on a large baking sheet so there is space between the potatoes. Place on the grill and roast for 45 minutes to 1 hour, until crispy skinned. Toss once during cooking. Grill: 400 ˚F

3. To make the butter: Place it in a medium sized shallow mixing bowl. Use a wooden spoon or strong spatula to break it up and soften it even more. Sprinkle the shallot, herbs, and salt over the butter, then use the spoon to combine the ingredients. Taste, adding more salt or herbs if necessary. Reserve a few tablespoons of the butter to serve on the potatoes.

4. To freeze the butter for future use, place a foot long piece of plastic wrap on the counter. Spread the butter out into a 6" log across the long direction of the plastic wrap towards the bottom. Begin to roll the plastic wrap away from you to roll it into a log, twisting the sides of the plastic wrap like a candy wrapper to secure.

5. Using your hands, shape the log into an even cylinder. Once it's wrapped tightly, place in the freezer. Then when more is needed, simply slice off coins of it to serve over grilled steak, chicken, veggies, or roasted potatoes. The butter holds well in the freezer for up to one month. Enjoy! *Cook times will vary depending on set and ambient temperatures.

Grilled Chili-lime Corn

Servings: 8
Cooking Time: 45 Minutes

Ingredients:

- 12 Corn, ears
- 1 Teaspoon chili powder
- 1/2 Teaspoon onion powder
- 1 Teaspoon Leinenkugel's Summer Shandy Rub
- 2 lime, juiced
- 1 Tablespoon lime zest

Directions:

1. Soak the ears of corn, still in their husk, in water for 4 to 8 hours.

2. Supply your smoker with wood pellets and follow the start-up procedure. Preheat the grill, with the lid closed, to 350° F.

3. Place corn directly on grill grates. Turn corn every 15 minutes for 45 minutes total cooking time. Grill: 350 ˚F

4. Combine chili powder, onion powder, Summer Shandy rub, lime juice, lime zest and butter in an oven safe dish and place in grill for

10 minutes. Remove corn and butter from the grill.

5. Pull corn husk back, but not off and remove corn silk. Using the corn husk as a handle, brush the corn with the melted chili-lime butter. Enjoy!

Roasted Hasselback Potatoes By Doug Scheiding

Servings: 6
Cooking Time: 120 Minutes

Ingredients:

- 6 Large russet potatoes
- 1 Pound bacon
- 1/2 Cup butter
- salt
- black pepper
- 1 Cup cheddar cheese
- 3 Whole scallions

Directions:

1. To cut potatoes, place two wooden spoons on either side of the potato (this prevents your knife from going all the way through). Slice potato into thin chips leaving about 1/4" attached on the bottom.

2. Freeze bacon slices for about 30 minutes then cut into small pieces about the size of a stamp. Place these in the cracks between every other slice.

3. Place the potato in a large cast iron skillet. Top the potato with slices of hard butter (you can also place thin slivers of cold butter between the potato slices with the bacon if desired). Season with salt and pepper.

4. Supply your smoker with wood pellets and follow the start-up procedure. Preheat the grill, with the lid closed, to 350° F.

5. Place the cast iron directly on the grill grate and cook for two hours. Top potatoes with more butter and baste with melted butter every 30 minutes.

6. In the last 10 minutes of cooking, sprinkle with cheddar and return to grill to melt.

7. To finish, top with chives or scallions. Enjoy!

Roasted Sheet Pan Vegetables

Servings: 4
Cooking Time: 25 Minutes

Ingredients:

- 1 Small head purple cauliflower, stemmed and cut into 2 inch florets
- 1 Small head yellow cauliflower, stemmed and cut into 2 inch florets
- 4 Cup butternut squash
- 2 Cup oyster or shiitake mushrooms, rinsed and sliced
- 3 Tablespoon olive oil
- 2 Teaspoon kosher salt
- freshly ground black pepper
- 1/4 Cup chopped flat-leaf parsley

Directions:

1. Supply your smoker with wood pellets and follow the start-up procedure. Preheat the grill, with the lid closed, to 450° F.

2. In a large mixing bowl, combine all of the vegetables. Drizzle olive oil over the top, along

with kosher salt and a generous grinding of black pepper.

3. Using your hands, toss the vegetables until they are evenly coated.

4. Spread out onto 1 or 2 half sheet pans or baking sheets, ensuring there is a little space between the veggies. (If they are too crowded, the vegetables will steam instead of roast and you won't get that crispy texture.)

5. Place the sheet pans on the grill and cook for 15 minutes. Open and stir, then close the lid and continue to cook until the vegetables are brown around the edges, about 5 to 15 minutes longer. Grill: 450 °F

6. Toss with parsley and serve immediately. The vegetables are also delicious at room temperature. Enjoy!

BEEF LAMB AND GAME RECIPES

Cucumber Beef Kefta

Servings: 4

Cooking Time: 10 Minutes

Ingredients:

- bamboo skewers, soaked in warm water
- 1 tbsp blackened saskatchewan rub seasoning
- 3 tbsp cilantro, chopped
- for topping, cucumbers
- 1 tsp cumin
- 2 lbs ground beef
- 1 tsp paprika
- 3 tbsp parsley, chopped
- pitas
- 1 red onion, grated
- for topping, tomatoes
- to taste, tzatziki sauce

Directions:

1. In a mixing bowl, combine ground beef, onion, Blackened Saskatchewan, cumin, paprika, cilantro, and parsley. Mix well, then cover and refrigerate for 1 hour to allow the flavors to blend.

2. Supply your smoker with wood pellets and follow the start-up procedure. Preheat the grill, with the lid closed, to 425° F. If using a gas or charcoal grill, set it up for medium-high heat.

3. Prepare kebabs: take small amounts of ground beef kefta and shape into popsicle-size cylinders. Skewer the meat, squeezing it to mold it to the skewer.

4. Grill kefta 3 to 5 minutes per side, then remove from the grill and serve warm with pitas, tzatziki sauce, and your favorite fresh veggies.

Salt-crusted Prime Rib

Servings: 8

Cooking Time: 180 Minutes

Ingredients:

- 1 1/2 Cup Jacobsen Salt Co. Pure Kosher Sea Salt
- 3/4 Cup coarse ground black pepper
- 1 Head garlic, peeled
- 1/2 Cup rosemary
- 2 Tablespoon chile powder
- 3/4 Cup extra-virgin olive oil
- 1 (15-16 lb) 6-bone prime rib roast

Directions:

1. In a food processor, combine salt, pepper, garlic cloves, rosemary and chile powder and process until fine. Add the olive oil and pulse to form a paste.

2. Place the prime rib roast on a cutting board, bone-side up and rub with 1 tablespoon of the salt paste.

3. Transfer the meat to a large roasting pan and place bone-side down. Pack the salt paste all over the fatty surface, pressing to help it adhere. Let the prime rib stand at room temperature for 1 hour.

4. Supply your smoker with wood pellets and follow the start-up procedure. Preheat the grill, with the lid closed, to 450° F.

5. Roast the prime rib for 1 hour, or until the crust is slightly darkened. Lower the Traeger temperature to 300°F and roast for about 2 hours and 15 minutes longer, or until an instant-read thermometer inserted into the center of the roast

(not touching the bone) registers 125°F for medium-rare. Grill: 450 °F

6. Transfer the roast to a large carving board and let the meat rest for 30 minutes. Grill: 300 °F Probe: 135 °F

7. Carefully lift the salt crust off the meat and transfer to a bowl. Brush away any excess salt.

8. To remove the roast in one piece while keeping the rib rack intact, run a long sharp carving knife along the bones, using them as your guide. Leave on 1/2 inch of meat, or more if reserving for leftovers.

9. Carve the prime rib roast 1/2 inch thick and serve, using some of the crumbled salt crust as a condiment.

Blackened Saskatchewan Tomahawk Steaks

Servings: 4
Cooking Time: 45 Minutes

Ingredients:
- 2 Whole tomahawk steaks
- 4 Tablespoon Blackened Saskatchewan Rub
- 2 Tablespoon butter

Directions:
1. Supply your smoker with wood pellets and follow the start-up procedure. Preheat the grill, with the lid closed, to 225° F.

2. Cover cold steaks in the Blackened Saskatchewan Rub. Let rest 10 minutes for the seasoning to adhere.

3. Place steaks directly on grill grates and smoke for about 40 minutes, or until an internal temp reaches 119°F. Remove from grill and wrap tightly in foil to rest.

4. Turn up temperature on the grill to 400°F - with a cast iron pan or griddle inside. When the pan is hot, add 2 Tbsp of butter and sear the first steak, about 2-4 minutes per side, or until the internal temperature reads 125°F - 130°F. Repeat with the other Tomahawk. Rest, slice, serve. Enjoy!

Smoked Duck Breast Bacon

Servings: 6
Cooking Time: 30 Minutes

Ingredients:
- 4 Cup water
- 2 Cup freshly brewed strong coffee
- 1 Cup kosher salt
- 1/2 Cup dark brown sugar
- 2 1/2 Tablespoon curing salt
- 1/4 Cup molasses
- 3 Cup ice
- 3 Pound skin-on duck breasts

Directions:
1. Stir together 4 cups water with coffee, kosher salt, brown sugar, and curing salt in a container with a lid. Mix until solids are dissolved. Add the molasses and stir until completely dissolved. Add 3 cups ice and stir until cure is cold. (It's ok if all the ice doesn't melt completely.)

2. Add duck breasts to cure and weigh them down with a large plate to keep submerged. Place covered container in refrigerator for a minimum of 6 hours.

3. Remove from refrigerator, take breasts out of brine and discard brine. Rinse duck breasts under cold running water and pat dry.

4. Supply your smoker with wood pellets and follow the start-up procedure. Preheat the grill, with the lid closed, to 165° F.

5. Place duck breasts on grill grate and smoke for 2 hours. Grill: 165 °F

6. Cool duck completely, wrap in plastic wrap and place in refrigerator until ready to use.

7. To cook, slice breast thinly and fry in a pan just like you would pork bacon. Or slice breast thinly, place on Traeger set to 350°F and cook for 10 minutes per side. Enjoy! Grill: 350 °F

Savory Reverse Seared Ny Steak

Servings: 4
Cooking Time: 68 Minutes

Ingredients:
- 4 Tbsp Butter
- Steak Seasoning
- 4 - 1 1/2" Steak, New York Strip

Directions:
1. Supply your smoker with wood pellets and follow the start-up procedure. Preheat the grill, with the lid closed, to 250° F.
2. As the grill is preheating to the perfect temperature, spice the steaks with the Chop House steak rub.
3. Lay the steaks on the grill for roughly 60 minutes or until the steaks reach an internal temperature of 105 to 110 degrees F. Remove the steaks and set aside.
4. Crank up the heat to 500°F, open the Flame Broiler plate and let the grill preheat.
5. Place the steaks back on the grill and sear for 4 minutes. Don't forget to add 1 TBSP of butter for flavor to each steak. You know when your steak is done once the internal temperature reaches 130 to 135°F (for medium-rare). Follow the below internal temperature for your cooking preference:
6. Rare: 125°F
7. Medium Rare: 130°F
8. Medium: 140°F
9. Well Done: 160°F
10. Once reached for personal preference, take the steaks off the grill and let them rest for 5 to 10 minutes before eating. ENJOY!

Delicious Barbecue Beef Brisket

Servings: 12
Cooking Time: 480 Minutes

Ingredients:
- 1 Beef Soup, Campbells Can
- 1 - 12 To 14 Lb Packer Beef, Brisket

Directions:
1. The night before you plan on cooking the brisket, trim the surface fat off the brisket with your sharp boning knife. Trim to leave about 1/8 to ¼ in fat.
2. Place the brisket in an unscented trash bag or on a sheet pan fat side up and season the meat side liberally with your favorite Rub. Let rest on the counter for 30 minutes until the rub is all soaked up. Flip the brisket over and season the fat side liberally. Cover or wrap up the brisket and put in the fridge overnight.
3. Prep your Grill by cleaning the grates, grease tray and firepot is clean. Supply your smoker with wood pellets and follow the start-up procedure. Preheat the grill, with the lid closed, to 250° F.
4. When grill has settled to 250°F place brisket in center of grill fat side down and cook for 4 hours.
5. After 4 hours, insert the meat probe into the fat seam between the point and flat so the end of the meat probe is in the center of the fat seam and continue to cook for about 2 more hours.
6. Prep aluminum foil to wrap the brisket in by tearing off 4 sheets of foil at least twice as large as

the brisket. Plus one more piece about the same size as the brisket.

7. When the meat thermometer reads 150°F to 160°F wrap the brisket in foil by placing the brisket fat side down on 2 sheets of foil. The cover with the other 2 sheets of foil and tightly roll/fold 3 sides up to seal – leaving one side open. Leave the meat probe in place in the brisket and lay the probe wire between the bottom and top foil sheets. Roll/fold the meat probe wire between the foil sheets as you are closing the foil. Dump the can of Campbell's Beef Consume into the foil through the open end and roll/fold that end closed.

8. Place the small foil sheet on the grill grate and place the foil-wrapped brisket on the small foil sheet on the grate. The small foil sheet will prevent the foil from sticking to the grate to prevent the foil from ripping and losing the foil juice that you can use later.

9. Continue to cook until the meat thermometer reads 200°F. Then unwrap one or two sides of the foil being careful not to lose any of the liquid in the foil. Insert a dinner fork into the flat portion of the brisket – if it goes in and out like a hot knife through butter it is done, if it has very much resistance, seal the sides of the foil and place back in grill and cook until the meat thermometer reads 205°F and test for tenderness again.

10. When the brisket is done, remove from grill, wrap in a clean towel and place in a small clean cooler to rest for at least 2 hours.

11. When ready to slice, remove brisket from foil. Separate the point end from the flat end by running your slicing knife down the fat seam. Slice the brisket across the grain into slices just thick enough to hold together.

12. Cube the point section into ½ in sq cubes by slicing ½ in slices across the grain first and then ½ in slices with the grain.

13. Place all slices and cubes into a pan and pour some of the liquid from the foil over the brisket.

14. Serve with your favorite BBQ Sauce on the side.

New York Strip Steaks With Blue Cheese Butter

Servings: 4

Cooking Time: 8 Minutes

Ingredients:

- 4 boneless New York strip steaks, each about 12oz (340g) and 1 inch (2.5cm) thick
- coarse salt
- freshly ground black pepper
- for the butter
- 8 tbsp unsalted butter, at room temperature
- 1 garlic clove, peeled and finely minced
- ⅓ cup crumbled blue cheese, mashed with a fork
- 1 tbsp minced chives
- 1 tsp Worcestershire sauce
- ½ tsp fresh coarsely ground black pepper

Directions:

1. Approximately 45 minutes before you're ready to cook, lightly season the steaks on both sides with salt and pepper. Place the steaks on a wire rack on a rimmed sheet pan.

2. Supply your smoker with wood pellets and follow the start-up procedure. Preheat the grill, with the lid closed, to 450° F.

3. In a small bowl, make the blue cheese butter by combining the ingredients. Mix thoroughly. Set aside.

4. Place the steaks on the grate at an angle to the bars. Sear until the internal temperature reaches 130°F (54°C), about 3 to 4 minutes per side, turning once.

5. Transfer the steaks to a platter and immediately top with a spoonful of room temperature blue cheese butter. Tent the steaks with aluminum foil for 2 to 3 minutes to encourage the butter to melt before serving.

Traeger Bbq Brisket

Servings: 8
Cooking Time: 540 Minutes

Ingredients:
- 1 (12-14 lb) whole packer brisket, trimmed
- Beef Rub

Directions:
1. Coat meat liberally with Traeger Beef Rub. When seasoned, wrap brisket in plastic wrap. Transfer wrapped brisket to the refrigerator and let sit for 12 to 24 hours.

2. Supply your smoker with wood pellets and follow the start-up procedure. Preheat the grill, with the lid closed, to 225° F.

3. Remove brisket from plastic wrap and place fat side down on the grill grate. Cook for 6 hours or until internal temperature reaches 160°F. Grill: 225 °F Probe: 160 °F

4. Remove brisket from the grill and wrap in a double layer of foil.

5. Place foiled brisket back on grill and cook until it reaches a finished internal temperature of 204°F, this should take an additional 3 to 4 hours. Grill: 225 °F Probe: 204 °F

6. Remove from grill and rest in the foil for at least 30 minutes. Slice against the grain. Enjoy!

Grilled Garlic Tomahawk Steak

Servings: 1 - 2
Cooking Time: 60 Minutes

Ingredients:
- 3 Tablespoons Unsalted Butter
- 2 Tablespoons Chophouse Steak Seasoning
- 2 Garlic, Cloves
- Kosher Salt
- 1 Sprig Rosemary, Fresh
- 1, 2-Inch Thick Bone-In Tomahawk Ribeye

Directions:
1. Supply your smoker with wood pellets and follow the start-up procedure. Preheat the grill, with the lid closed, to 225° F.

2. Generously coat the tomahawk steak with kosher salt on all sides.

3. Allow the steak to sit at room temperature for one hour. After an hour, wipe off the salt and pat the steak dry.

4. Season the tomahawk steak with Chophouse Steak on both sides.

5. Place the steak on the grill grates, insert a temperature probe, and grill, undisturbed, for 45 minutes, or until the steak reaches an internal temperature of 120°F.

6. Remove the steak from the grill, tent with aluminum foil and allow it to rest for 10 minutes.

7. Place a cast iron skillet on the grill and increase the temperature of the   to 450°F. Allow the pan to get as hot as possible.

8. Place the steak in the cast iron pan with the butter, garlic cloves, and rosemary sprig. Immediately begin spooning the butter over the steak as it melts.

9. Sear on one side for 1 minute.

10. Flip the steak, place the garlic and rosemary on top of the steak, and continue to baste the steak with the butter for another minute.

11. Pull the steak off the grill and allow it to rest for 10 minutes until the temperature rises to 130-135°F.

12. Pour the melted butter from the pan over the steak, slice, and serve immediately.

Flavour Smoked Chuck Roast

Servings: 6
Cooking Time: 540 Minutes

Ingredients:
- 3 cups beef stock, divided
- 1, 3 lb chuck roast
- 3 tbsp sweet heat rub
- 1 yellow onion

Directions:
1. Place chuck roast in a 9x13 baking pan. Sprinkle generously with   Sweet Heat Rub and rub to coat evenly on all sides.

2. Cover pan with foil and refrigerate overnight.

3. The next day, remove chuck roast from refrigerator and let it come to room temperature.

4. Supply your smoker with wood pellets and follow the start-up procedure. Preheat the grill, with the lid closed, to 225° F. If using a gas or charcoal grill, set it for low heat.

5. Insert a temperature probe into the thickest side of the roast, then place chuck roast directly on grill grate. Close lid and smoke for 3 hours.

6. Spray roast with 1 cup of beef stock every hour.

7. Slice the onion and place in a 9x13 aluminum pan. Pour the remaining cup of stock over the onions and set roast on top of onions.

8. Increase temperature to 250°F and cook an additional 2 ½ to 3 hours, or until internal temperature reaches 165°F.

9. Once 165°F internal temperature is reached, cover roast with aluminum foil, and cook another 2 ½ to 3 hours, or until internal temperature reaches 200°F.

10. Remove chuck roast from grill.

11. Allow roast to rest 15 minutes, then remove from pan and shred with meat claws. For added moistness and flavor, pour some remaining cooking stock over the shredded roast and serve.

Bourbon-braised Beef Short Ribs

Servings: 4
Cooking Time: 180 Minutes

Ingredients:
- 1/2 Cup yellow mustard
- 2 Tablespoon Worcestershire sauce
- 1 Tablespoon molasses
- 12 beef short ribs, preferably from the chuck or plate
- Prime Rib Rub
- 1 Cup beef broth
- 3 Tablespoon soy sauce or Bragg Liquid Aminos
- 2 Tablespoon bourbon

Directions:
1. Supply your smoker with wood pellets and follow the start-up procedure. Preheat the grill, with the lid closed, to 250° F.

2. In a small mixing bowl, combine mustard, Worcestershire sauce and molasses; whisk to mix.

3. Coat each rib on all sides with the mustard slather sauce. Season with Traeger Prime Rib Rub.

4. Make the mop sauce: Combine the beef broth, soy sauce and bourbon in a food-safe spray bottle.

5. Place the short ribs, bone-side down, directly on the grill grate. Cook for 2 to 2-1/2 hours, or until the internal temperature of each rib is 165°F when read on an instant-read meat thermometer, spraying with the mop sauce every 30 minutes. Grill: 250 °F Probe: 165 °F

6. Transfer the ribs to a large sheet of heavy-duty aluminum foil. Bring up the edges of the foil and add whatever remains of the mop sauce. Bring the opposite sides of the foil together and fold several times, tightly enclosing the ribs. Return the foil-enclosed ribs to the grill grate.

7. Continue to cook the ribs until the internal temperature is 195°F, about 1 hour more. Grill: 250 °F Probe: 195 °F

8. Let the ribs rest for 15 minutes, still enclosed in the foil, then open carefully. (Watch out for escaping steam.) Transfer the ribs to a platter or plates, then drizzle with the juices.

Flavour Memphis Bbq Beef Brisket

Servings: 10
Cooking Time: 600 Minutes

Ingredients:

- 1 Cup Beef Broth
- 1, 10-12 Pound Brisket
- 1 Bottle Sweet Rib Rub

Directions:

1. Cut away any silver skin or excess fat from the flat muscle and discard. Next, there will be a large, crescent shaped fat section on the flat of the meat.

2. Trim that fat until it is smooth against the meat so that it looks like a seamless transition between the point and flat. Flip the brisket over and trim the fat cap to ¼ inch thick. Slice between the point and the flat and save the flat for later.

3. Generously season the trimmed brisket point on all sides with the Sweet Rib Rub. Allow the brisket to sit for 30 minutes to marinate.

4. Pour the beef broth in the spray bottle and set aside.

5. Supply your smoker with wood pellets and follow the start-up procedure. Preheat the grill, with the lid closed, to 225° F. Place the brisket in the smoker, insert the smoker's attached temperature probe, if you have one, and set the brisket to cook for about 6-8 hours or until the internal temperature reaches 165°F. Spray the brisket with the beef broth every 2 hours to keep it moist.

6. Once the brisket reaches 165°F, remove from the smoker, wrap in peach butcher paper, folding the edges over to form a leakproof seal, and return to the smoker seam-side down for another 3-4 hours, or until the brisket reaches 200°F.

7. Remove the brisket from the smoker and allow it to rest for at least one hour before serving.

Grilled Rib Eyes With Hasselback Sweet Potatoes

Servings: 4
Cooking Time: 60 Minutes

Ingredients:

- 2 (1-1/2 to 2 lb) bone-in rib-eye steaks
- 4 sweet potatoes
- extra-virgin olive oil
- salt and pepper

Directions:

1. One hour before preparing, remove the steaks from the refrigerator to allow them to come to room temperature.

2. Supply your smoker with wood pellets and follow the start-up procedure. Preheat the grill, with the lid closed, to 400° F.

3. Place the cut potatoes on a sheet pan. Drizzle with oil and season generously with salt and pepper. Place the pan on the grill. Roast until the potatoes are browned on the outside and tender in the center, 50 to 60 minutes.

4. While the sweet potatoes are roasting, prep the steaks. Rub each steak with oil, and sprinkle salt and pepper generously over each side.

5. When the sweet potatoes are almost done, place the steaks on the grill and cook, allowing each side to sear, until the internal temperature reaches 130°F for medium-rare, 4 to 5 minutes per side. Grill: 400 °F Probe: 130 °F

6. Remove the steaks from the grill, and let rest for 10 minutes.

Irish Pasties

Servings: 4
Cooking Time: 20 Minutes

Ingredients:

- 1 Pound Roast Beef, cubed & browned
- 4 Whole Potatoes, cooked & cut into 1/2" cubes
- salt and pepper
- 1 Piecrust
- milk
- 2 Cup Beef Gravy

Directions:

1. Supply your smoker with wood pellets and follow the start-up procedure. Preheat the grill, with the lid closed, to 425° F.

2. Mix the beef, potatoes, salt, and pepper in a large mixing bowl. Unroll the piecrust, and cut in half. Put a good amount of filling in each half, fold over, and seal shut. Brush with a little milk.

3. Place on a greased basking sheet, and poke a few holes in the top of each pasty. Bake for 16-20 minutes, or until the crust is golden brown. Grill: 425 °F

4. Remove from the Traeger, brush with butter, and serve with gravy. Enjoy!

Grilled Rosemary Rack Of Lamb

Servings: 8
Cooking Time: 30 Minutes

Ingredients:

- 2 Tablespoons Dijon Mustard
- 1 Tablespoon Fresh Parsley, Chopped
- Chop House Steak Rub
- 2 Chine Bones Removed, And Excess Fat Trimmed Racks Of Lamb
- 1 Teaspoon Rosemary, Finely Chopped

Directions:

1. Place the racks of lamb on a flat work surface, then generously brush the lamb all over with Dijon mustard.

2. Season the meat on all sides with Chophouse Steak seasoning and sprinkle with parsley and rosemary.

3. Supply your smoker with wood pellets and follow the start-up procedure. Preheat the grill, with the lid closed, to 400° F.

4. If you're using a gas or charcoal grill, set it up for high heat.

5. Insert a temperature probe into the thickest part of the rack of lamb and sear the rack, meaty side down for about 6 minutes.

6. Remove the lamb from the grill and turn the temperature down to 300°F.

7. Return the lamb to the grill and lean the two racks against each other so that they stand up, and grill for another 20 minutes, or until the internal temperature reaches 130°F.

8. Remove the racks from the grill and allow to rest for 10 minutes before carving and serving.

Smoked Pheasant

Servings: 4-6
Cooking Time: 240 Minutes

Ingredients:

- 1 gallon hot water
- 1 cup salt
- 1 cup packed brown sugar
- 2 (2- to 3-pound) whole pheasants, cleaned and plucked
- ¼ cup extra-virgin olive oil
- 2 tablespoons onion powder
- 2 tablespoons freshly ground black pepper
- 2 tablespoons cayenne pepper
- 1 tablespoon minced garlic
- 2 teaspoons smoked paprika
- 1 cup molasses

Directions:

1. In a large container with a lid, combine the hot water, salt, and brown sugar, stirring to dissolve the salt and sugar. Let cool to room temperature, then submerge the pheasants in the brine, cover, and refrigerate for 8 to 12 hours.

2. Remove the pheasants from the brine, then rinse them and pat dry. Discard the brine.

3. Supply your smoker with wood pellets and follow the start-up procedure. Preheat, with the lid closed, to 250°F.

4. In a small bowl, combine the olive oil, black pepper, cayenne pepper, onion powder, garlic, and paprika to form a paste.

5. Rub the pheasants with the paste and place breast-side up on the grill grate. Close the lid and smoke for 1 hour.

6. Open the smoker and baste the pheasants with some of the molasses. Close the lid and continue smoking for 2 to 3 hours, basting with the molasses every 30 minutes, until a meat thermometer inserted into the thigh reads 160°F.

7. Remove the pheasants from the grill and let rest for 20 minutes before serving warm or cold.

Savory Smoked Brisket

Servings: 10
Cooking Time: 600 Minutes

Ingredients:

- 4 Tbsp Apple Cider Vinegar
- 10Lb Trimmed Brisket
- 2 Cups Broth, Beef
- Sweet Heat Rub
- 2 Tbsp Worcestershire Sauce

Directions:

1. Trim the fat cap from your brisket, leaving enough fat to baste the meat during the smoke process.

2. Generously coat the brisket with Sweet Heat rub, and massage into the brisket.

3. In a bowl, whisk together the apple cider vinegar, Worcestershire sauce and beef broth, then pour into a clean spray bottle.

4. Supply your smoker with wood pellets and follow the start-up procedure. Preheat the grill, with the lid closed, to 225° F. Once the smoker is up to temperature, place the brisket inside and insert the temperature probe. Smoke for 10 to 12

hours, or until the internal temperature of the brisket reaches 200°F at the thickest part. Once an hour, spray the brisket with the mop sauce to baste it.

5. Once the brisket is done, remove from the smoker, allow to rest for 30 minutes under tin foil, then slice and enjoy!

Smoked Seed Pastrami

Servings: 16
Cooking Time: 480 Minutes

Ingredients:

- For the brisket and brine:
- 1 beef brisket flat with plenty of fat intact (6 to 8 pounds)
- 2 quarts hot water and 2 quarts ice water
- 2/3 cup coarse salt (sea or kosher)
- 2 teaspoons pink curing salt (Prague Powder No. 1 or Insta Cure No. 1)
- 1 small onion, peeled and cut in half widthwise
- 8 cloves garlic, peeled and cut in half widthwise
- For the spice rub:
- 1/2 cup cracked black peppercorns
- 1/2 cup coriander seeds
- 2 tablespoons mustard seeds
- 1 tablespoon light or dark brown sugar
- 1 teaspoon ground ginger
- Beer (optional)

Directions:

1. Trim the brisket, leaving a fat cap on top at least 1/4 inch thick.

2. Make the brine: Place the hot water, coarse salt, and pink salt in a large bowl or plastic tub and whisk until the salt crystals are dissolved. Stir in the ice water, onion, and garlic. Place the brisket in a jumbo heavy-duty resealable plastic bag. Add the brine and seal the top, squeezing out the air as you go. Place in a second bag and seal, then place in an aluminum foil pan or roasting pan to contain any leaks. Brine the brisket in the refrigerator for 12 days, turning it over once a day.

3. Make the rub: Place the peppercorns, coriander seeds, mustard seeds, brown sugar, and ginger in a spice mill and grind to a coarse powder, running the machine in short bursts, working in batches as needed. The final rub should feel gritty like coarse sand.

4. Drain the brisket, rinse well under cold running water, and blot dry with paper towels. Place it on a rimmed baking sheet or in a roasting pan and thickly crust it on all sides with the rub.

5. Supply your smoker with wood pellets and follow the start-up procedure. Preheat the grill, with the lid closed, to 225 °F-250 °F. Fill an aluminum foil pan with water or beer to a depth of 3 inches and place it below the rack on which you'll be smoking the ribs.

6. Place the pastrami fat side up in the smoker, directly on the rack. Smoke the pastrami until crusty and black on the outside and cooked to 175 °F on an instant-read thermometer, 7 to 8 hours.

7. Wrap the pastrami in butcher paper. Return it to the smoker. Continue cooking until the internal temperature is 200 °F and the meat is tender enough to pierce with a gloved finger or wooden spoon handle, an additional 1 to 2 hours, or as needed. (You'll need to unwrap it to check it.)

8. Transfer the wrapped pastrami to an insulated cooler and let rest for 1 to 2 hours. Unwrap and slice crosswise (across the grain) for serving.

Smoked Teriyaki Jerky

Servings: 6
Cooking Time: 240 Minutes

Ingredients:

- 1/2 Cup soy sauce
- 1/4 Cup mirin or sweet cooking wine
- 2 Tablespoon sugar
- 3 coins fresh ginger, each ¼ inch thick
- 1 Clove garlic, crushed
- 1/2 Teaspoon onion powder
- 1/2 Teaspoon black pepper
- 2 Pound trimmed beef top or bottom round, sirloin tip, flank steak or wild game

Directions:

1. In a mixing bowl, combine soy sauce, mirin, sugar, ginger, garlic, onion powder and black pepper.

2. With a sharp knife, slice the beef into 1/4 inch thick slices with the grain. This is much easier to do if the meat is partially frozen. Trim off any fat or connective tissue.

3. Put the beef slices in a large resealable plastic bag and pour the marinade over the beef. Massage the bag so all the slices get coated with the marinade. Seal the bag and refrigerate for several hours or overnight.

4. Supply your smoker with wood pellets and follow the start-up procedure. Preheat the grill, with the lid closed, to 180° F.

5. Remove the beef from the marinade and discard the marinade.

6. Dry the beef slices between paper towels and arrange the meat in a single layer on the grill grate.

7. Smoke on the Traeger for 4 to 5 hours or until the jerky is dry but still pliant when bent. Grill: 180 ˚F

8. Immediately transfer the jerky to a resealable plastic bag and let it rest for an hour at room temperature.

9. Squeeze the air out of the bag and keep the jerky in the refrigerator. Enjoy!

Easy Breakfast Cheeseburger

Servings: 2
Cooking Time: 10 Minutes

Ingredients:

- 4 Bacon, Strip
- 6 Ounce Lean Beef, Ground
- 2 Burger Buns
- 2 Cheese, Sliced
- 2 Egg
- Pepper
- Salt

Directions:

1. Supply your smoker with wood pellets and follow the start-up procedure. Preheat the grill, with the lid closed, to 400° F.

2. Take the ground beef and divide it into two thin patties. Brush the grate with oil, then add the patties and grill them on about 2-5 minutes on each side, or until the desired doneness, pressing down to get a good sear.

3. Remove the burgers from the grill, then build your burger. Starting with the bottom bun or bread slice, add the patty, then a slice of American cheese, top with bacon, hash browns, an egg over easy, and finish with the top bun or bread slice. Now it's ready to serve!

Italian Meatballs

Servings: 6
Cooking Time: 90 Minutes

Ingredients:

- 1lb (450g) ground beef (85/15), well chilled
- ½lb (225g) Italian sausage, well chilled
- 1 large egg, beaten
- ½ cup finely grated Parmesan, Asiago, or Romano cheese
- ½ cup panko or other breadcrumbs
- 1 tsp Italian seasoning
- 1 tsp coarse salt
- ½ tsp freshly ground black pepper
- 1lb (450g) thin-sliced bacon, halved crosswise
- low-carb barbecue sauce, (optional)

Directions:

1. Supply your smoker with wood pellets and follow the start-up procedure. Preheat the grill, with the lid closed, to 250° F.

2. Place the ground beef, Italian sausage, egg, cheese, breadcrumbs, Italian seasoning, and salt and pepper in a large bowl. Wet your hands with cold water. Form your hands into claw shapes and combine the ingredients using a light touch.

3. Form the mixture into 24 equal-sized balls. Wrap each with a half strip of bacon and secure the ends with a toothpick.

4. Place the meatballs on the grate and smoke until the bacon has rendered its fat and the internal temperature reaches 160°F (71°C), about 1 to 1½ hours. Brush the meatballs with barbecue sauce (if using) during the last 10 minutes of smoking.

5. Transfer the meatballs to a platter. Let rest for 5 minutes before serving.

Texas Smoked Brisket

Servings: 12-15
Cooking Time: 960 Minutes

Ingredients:

- 1 (12-pound) full packer brisket
- 2 tablespoons yellow mustard
- 1 batch Espresso Brisket Rub
- Worcestershire Mop and Spritz, for spritzing

Directions:

1. Supply your smoker with wood pellets and follow the start-up procedure. Preheat the grill, with the lid closed, to 225°F.

2. Using a boning knife, carefully remove all but about ½ inch of the large layer of fat covering one side of your brisket.

3. Coat the brisket all over with mustard and season it with the rub. Using your hands, work the rub into the meat. Pour the mop into a spray bottle.

4. Place the brisket directly on the grill grate and smoke until its internal temperature reaches 195°F, spritzing it every hour with the mop.

5. Pull the brisket from the grill and wrap it completely in aluminum foil or butcher paper. Place the wrapped brisket in a cooler, cover the cooler, and let it rest for 1 or 2 hours.

6. Remove the brisket from the cooler and unwrap it.

7. Separate the brisket point from the flat by cutting along the fat layer and slice the flat. The point can be saved for burnt ends (see Sweet Heat Burnt Ends), or sliced and served as well.

Jalapeño Beef Jerky

Servings: 8
Cooking Time: 240 Minutes

Ingredients:

- 2 jalapeños, stemmed and seeded (or leave seeds in for a hotter jerky)
- 1/4 Cup lime juice
- 1/4 Cup soy sauce
- 4 Tablespoon brown sugar
- 1 Cup Mexican beer
- 2 Tablespoon Morton Tender Quick Home Meat Cure
- 2 Pound beef top or bottom round, sirloin tip, flank steak or wild game

Directions:

1. In a blender or small food processor, combine the jalapeños, lime juice, soy sauce, curing salt and brown sugar and process until the jalapeño is finely chopped. Set aside.

2. With a sharp knife, trim any fat or connective tissue from the meat. Slice the beef into 1/4 inch thick slices against the grain. (This is easier if the meat is partially frozen.)

3. Place the beef slices in a large resealable bag. Transfer jalapeño mixture to the resealable bag and top with beer. Massage the bag so that all the slices get coated with the marinade. Seal and refrigerate for several hours, or overnight.

4. Supply your smoker with wood pellets and follow the start-up procedure. Preheat the grill, with the lid closed, to 180° F.

5. Remove the beef from the marinade and discard the marinade. Dry the beef slices between paper towels. Arrange the meat in a single layer directly on the grill grate. Grill: 180 ˚F

6. Smoke for 4 to 5 hours, or until the jerky is dry but still chewy and somewhat pliant when you bend a piece. Grill: 180 ˚F

7. Transfer to a cooling rack and rest for an hour at room temperature.

8. Store in a resealable bag. Squeeze any air from the bag, and refrigerate the jerky. It will keep for several weeks in the fridge.

Smoked Beef Back Ribs

Servings: 6
Cooking Time: 480 Minutes

Ingredients:

- 2 Rack beef back ribs
- 1/2 Cup Beef Rub

Directions:

1. If your butcher has not already done so, remove the thin papery membrane from the bone-side of the ribs by working the tip of a butter knife underneath the membrane over a middle bone. Use paper towels to get a firm grip, then tear the membrane off.

2. Season both sides of ribs with Traeger Beef Rub.

3. Supply your smoker with wood pellets and follow the start-up procedure. Preheat the grill, with the lid closed, to 225° F.

4. Arrange the ribs on the grill grate, bone side down. Cook for 8-10 hours, or until internal temperature reaches 205˚F. Grill: 225 ˚F Probe: 205 ˚F

5. Remove ribs from grill and let rest, lightly covered for 20 minutes before slicing and serving. Enjoy!

Smoked Beer Corned Beef

Servings: 6
Cooking Time: 240 Minutes

Ingredients:

- 6 lb corned beef brisket raw
- 2 tbsp black pepper
- 8 oz light beer

Directions:

1. Supply your smoker with wood pellets and follow the start-up procedure. Preheat the grill, with the lid closed, to 275 °F.
2. Cut open packaging of corned beef and drain off liquid. Be sure to grab the spice packet included with the brisket. Gently rinse off corned beef and then pat dry with a paper towel.
3. Open the spice packet included with your corned beef and sprinkle contents over the brisket, then sprinkle a light dusting of black pepper according to your preference.
4. Once pellet grill has reached temperature, insert probes into corned beef brisket pieces. If you only have a single probe, insert that probe in the center of the smallest piece because it will cook the fastest.
5. Smoke for 3 to 4 hours until corned beef reaches an internal temperature of 175 degrees F. Next transfer briskets to an aluminum pan and pour just enough beer in to cover the bottom of the pan. Cover with foil leaving one corner open to let out steam.
6. Continue cooking for another 2-3 hours until internal temperature reaches about 205 degrees F. Use an instant read thermometer and poke different parts of the brisket checking for tenderness. If probe goes into the meat with very little tension than it is done. If not, continue cooking until it becomes tender.
7. Once meat is tender and fully cooked, remove pan from pellet grill and let the corned beef rest for about 30 minutes still covered with one corner open to prevent overcooking.
8. Slice corned beef into 1/8 inch slices cutting against the grains of the brisket. If brisket crumbles make slices a little thicker.

Garlic Cheese Bacon Burger

Servings: 7
Cooking Time: 16 Minutes

Ingredients:

- 14 Bacon, Strip
- 3 Lbs Chuck Beef, Ground
- 7 Burger Buns
- 4 Cloves Garlic, Minced
- 1 Onion, Chopped
- 1 Tsp Pepper
- 8 Oz Pepper Jack Cheese, Sliced
- 2 Tomato, Sliced

Directions:

1. Supply your smoker with wood pellets and follow the start-up procedure. Preheat the grill, with the lid closed, to 400° F.
2. In a bowl, mix together the ground chuck, garlic, onion, and pepper. Separate the beef mixtures into about 7 equal bundles and form hamburger patties.
3. Brush the grate with oil, then add the patties and grill them on about 5-8 minutes on each side, or until desired doneness.
4. Remove the burgers from the grill. On the bottom half of the burger bun, add two tomato slices, top with a slice of pepper jack cheese, add the patty,
5. Place another slice of cheese on top, add two slices of bacon and top it off with the other half of the burger bun and serve.

Mesquite Smoked Brisket

Servings: 8-12
Cooking Time: 720 Minutes

Ingredients:

- 1 (12-pound) full packer brisket
- 2 tablespoons yellow mustard (you can also use soy sauce)
- Salt
- Freshly ground black pepper

Directions:

1. Supply your smoker with wood pellets and follow the start-up procedure. Preheat the grill, with the lid closed, to 225°F.
2. Using a boning knife, carefully remove all but about ½ inch of the large layer of fat covering one side of your brisket.
3. Coat the brisket all over with mustard and season it with salt and pepper.
4. Place the brisket directly on the grill grate and smoke until its internal temperature reaches 160°F and the brisket has formed a dark bark.
5. Pull the brisket from the grill and wrap it completely in aluminum foil or butcher paper.
6. Increase the grill's temperature to 350°F and return the wrapped brisket to it. Continue to cook until its internal temperature reaches 190°F.
7. Transfer the wrapped brisket to a cooler, cover the cooler, and let the brisket rest for 1 or 2 hours.
8. Remove the brisket from the cooler and unwrap it.
9. Separate the brisket point from the flat by cutting along the fat layer, and slice the flat. The point can be saved for burnt ends (see Sweet Heat Burnt Ends), or sliced and served as well.

Baked Ziti With Italian Sausage

Servings: 6
Cooking Time: 20 Minutes

Ingredients:

- 1 Pound Ziti, cooked 1 minute less than directions, and dried
- 1 Jar Spaghetti Sauce
- 1 Teaspoon garlic, minced
- 1 Pinch red pepper flakes
- 1 Pound Italian Sausage, cooked
- salt and pepper
- 2 Cup Mozzarella Cheese, Grated
- 1/4 Cup Parmesan cheese

Directions:

1. Supply your smoker with wood pellets and follow the start-up procedure. Preheat the grill, with the lid closed, to 450° F.
2. In a large bowl, pour your spaghetti sauce over the cooked pasta, add garlic, red pepper flakes, and salt and pepper to taste. Toss. Fold the sausage into the pasta mixture.
3. Coat a 9 x 13 x 2-inch baking dish with nonstick cooking spray.
4. Pour half of the pasta mixture into your prepared baking dish. Sprinkle with half of the mozzarella. Pour remaining pasta into the dish, smooth out the top and add the remaining mozzarella.
5. Bake in Traeger until cheese is golden brown and bubbly, about 20 minutes.
6. Remove and sprinkle with parmesan cheese. Enjoy!

Traeger Bacon-wrapped Filet Mignon

Servings: 2
Cooking Time: 15 Minutes

Ingredients:

- 3 (6 oz) filet mignon steaks
- 1 Teaspoon pepper
- 1 Teaspoon salt
- 2 Clove garlic, minced
- 3 Tablespoon butter, softened
- 3 Slices bacon

Directions:

1. Filets don't have much marbling, so when selecting meat look for a rich red color.

2. In a small bowl, combine salt, pepper, garlic and softened butter. Rub on both sides of filet. Let rest 10 minutes.

3. Supply your smoker with wood pellets and follow the start-up procedure. Preheat the grill, with the lid closed, to 450° F.

4. Wrap each steak in a slice of bacon and secure with a toothpick.

5. Place steaks directly on the grill and cook for 5 to 8 minutes on each side, or until the filets reach an internal temperature of 130°F for medium-rare. Enjoy! Grill: 450 °F Probe: 130 °F

Chicken Wings With Teriyaki Glaze

Servings: 4
Cooking Time: 50 Minutes

Ingredients:

- 16 large chicken wings, about 3lb (1.4kg) total
- 1 to 1½ tbsp toasted sesame oil
- for the glaze
- ½ cup light soy sauce or tamari
- ¼ cup sake or sugar-free dark-colored soda
- ¼ cup light brown sugar or low-carb substitute
- 2 tbsp mirin or 1 tbsp honey
- 1 garlic clove, peeled, minced or grated
- 2 tsp minced fresh ginger
- 1 tsp cornstarch mixed with 1 tbsp distilled water (optional)
- for serving
- 1 tbsp toasted sesame seeds
- 2 scallions, trimmed, white and green parts sliced sharply diagonally

Directions:

1. Supply your smoker with wood pellets and follow the start-up procedure. Preheat the grill, with the lid closed, to 350° F.

2. Place the chicken wings in a large bowl, add the sesame oil, and turn the wings to coat thoroughly.

3. Place the wings on the grate at an angle to the bars. Grill for 20 minutes and then turn. Continue to cook until the wings are nicely browned and the meat is no longer pink at the bone, about 20 minutes more.

4. To make the glaze, in a saucepan on the stovetop over medium-high heat, combine the ingredients and bring the mixture to a boil. Reduce the glaze by 1/3, about 6 to 8 minutes. If you prefer your glaze to be glossy and thick, add the cornstarch and water mixture to the glaze and cook until it coats the back of a spoon, about 1 to 2 minutes more.

5. Transfer the wings to an aluminum foil roasting pan. Pour the glaze over them, turning to coat thoroughly. Place the pan on the grate and cook the wings until the glaze sets, about 5 to 10 minutes.

6. Transfer the wings to a platter. Scatter the sesame seeds and scallions over the top. Serve with plenty of napkins.

Bacon-wrapped Jalapeño Poppers

Servings: 12
Cooking Time: 30 Minutes

Ingredients:

- 8 ounces cream cheese, softened
- ½ cup shredded Cheddar cheese
- ¼ cup chopped scallions
- 1 teaspoon chipotle chile powder or regular chili powder
- 1 teaspoon garlic powder
- 1 teaspoon salt
- 18 large jalapeño peppers, stemmed, seeded, and halved lengthwise
- 1 pound bacon (precooked works well)

Directions:

1. Supply your smoker with wood pellets and follow the start-up procedure. Preheat, with the

lid closed, to 350°F. Line a baking sheet with aluminum foil.

2. In a small bowl, combine the cream cheese, Cheddar cheese, scallions, chipotle powder, garlic powder, and salt.

3. Stuff the jalapeño halves with the cheese mixture.

4. Cut the bacon into pieces big enough to wrap around the stuffed pepper halves.

5. Wrap the bacon around the peppers and place on the prepared baking sheet.

6. Put the baking sheet on the grill grate, close the lid, and smoke the peppers for 30 minutes, or until the cheese is melted and the bacon is cooked through and crisp.

7. Let the jalapeño poppers cool for 3 to 5 minutes. Serve warm.

Bacon Pork Pinwheels (kansas Lollipops)

Servings: 4-6
Cooking Time: 20 Minutes

Ingredients:
- 1 Whole Pork Loin, boneless
- To Taste salt and pepper
- To Taste Greek Seasoning
- 4 Slices bacon
- To Taste The Ultimate BBQ Sauce

Directions:
1. When ready to cook, start the smoker and set temperature to 500F. Preheat, lid closed, for 10 to 15 minutes.

2. Trim pork loin of any unwanted silver skin or fat. Using a sharp knife, cut pork loin length wise, into 4 long strips.

3. Lay pork flat, then season with salt, pepper and Cavender's Greek Seasoning.

4. Flip the pork strips over and layer bacon on unseasoned side. Begin tightly rolling the pork strips, with bacon being rolled up on the inside.

5. Secure a skewer all the way through each pork roll to secure it in place. Set the pork rolls down on grill and cook for 15 minutes.

6. Brush BBQ Sauce over the pork. Turn each skewer over, then coat the other side. Let pork cook for another 5-10 minutes, depending on thickness of your pork. Enjoy!

Bayou Wings With Cajun Rémoulade

Servings: 8
Cooking Time: 40 Minutes

Ingredients:
- 16 large whole chicken wings or 32 drumettes and flats, about 3lb (1.4kg) total
- for the rub
- 1 tbsp kosher salt
- 1 tsp freshly ground black pepper
- 1 tsp paprika
- ½ tsp ground cayenne, plus more
- ½ tsp garlic powder
- ½ tsp celery salt
- ½ tsp dried thyme
- 2 tbsp vegetable oil
- for the rémoulade
- 1¼ cups reduced-fat mayo
- ¼ cup Creole-style or whole grain mustard
- 2 tbsp horseradish
- 2 tbsp pickle relish
- 1 tbsp freshly squeezed lemon juice
- 1 tsp paprika, plus more
- 1 tsp hot sauce, plus more
- 1 tsp Worcestershire sauce
- coarse salt

- for serving
- lemon wedges
- pickled okra (optional)

Directions:

1. Supply your smoker with wood pellets and follow the start-up procedure. Preheat the grill, with the lid closed, to 350° F.

2. If using whole wings, cut through the two joints, separating them into drumettes, flats, and wing tips. (Discard the wing tips or save them for chicken stock.) Alternatively, leave the wings whole. Place the chicken in a resealable plastic bag.

3. In a small bowl, make the rub by combining the ingredients. Mix well. Pour the rub over the wings and toss them to thoroughly coat. Refrigerate for 2 hours.

4. In a small bowl, make the Cajun rémoulade by whisking together the mayo, mustard, horseradish, pickle relish, lemon juice, paprika, hot sauce, and Worcestershire. Season with salt to taste. The mixture should be highly seasoned. Transfer to a serving bowl and lightly dust with paprika. Cover and refrigerate until ready to serve.

5. Remove the wings from the refrigerator and allow the excess marinade to drip off. Place the wings on the grate at an angle to the bars. Grill for 20 minutes and then turn. (They'll brown more evenly but will also have less of a tendency to stick.) Continue to cook until the wings are nicely browned and the meat is no longer pink at the bone, about 20 minutes more.

6. Remove the wings from the grill and pile them on a platter. Serve with the Cajun rémoulade, lemon wedges, and pickled okra (if using).

Pulled Pork Loaded Nachos

Servings: 4
Cooking Time: 10 Minutes

Ingredients:

- 2 cups leftover smoked pulled pork
- 1 small sweet onion, diced
- 1 medium tomato, diced
- 1 jalapeño pepper, seeded and diced
- 1 garlic clove, minced
- 1 teaspoon salt
- 1 teaspoon freshly ground black pepper
- 1 bag tortilla chips
- 1 cup shredded Cheddar cheese
- ½ cup The Ultimate BBQ Sauce, divided
- ½ cup shredded jalapeño Monterey Jack cheese
- Juice of ½ lime
- 1 avocado, halved, pitted, and sliced
- 2 tablespoons sour cream
- 1 tablespoon chopped fresh cilantro

Directions:

1. Supply your smoker with wood pellets and follow the start-up procedure. Preheat, with the lid closed, to 375°F.

2. Heat the pulled pork in the microwave.

3. In a medium bowl, combine the onion, tomato, jalapeño, garlic, salt, and pepper, and set aside.

4. Arrange half of the tortilla chips in a large cast iron skillet. Spread half of the warmed pork on top and cover with the Cheddar cheese. Top with half of the onion-jalapeño mixture, then drizzle with ¼ cup of barbecue sauce.

5. Layer on the remaining tortilla chips, then the remaining pork and the Monterey Jack cheese. Top with the remaining onion-jalapeño mixture

and drizzle with the remaining ¼ cup of barbecue sauce.

6. Place the skillet on the grill, close the lid, and smoke for about 10 minutes, or until the cheese is melted and bubbly. (Watch to make sure your chips don't burn!)

7. Squeeze the lime juice over the nachos, top with the avocado slices and sour cream, and garnish with the cilantro before serving hot.

Citrus-infused Marinated Olives

Servings: 6
Cooking Time: 30 Minutes

Ingredients:

- 1½ cups mixed brined olives, with pits
- ½ cup extra virgin olive oil
- 1 tbsp freshly squeezed lemon juice
- 1 garlic clove, peeled and thinly sliced
- 1 tsp smoked Spanish paprika
- 2 sprigs of fresh rosemary
- 2 sprigs of fresh thyme
- 2 bay leaves, fresh or dried
- 1 small dried red chili pepper, deseeded and flesh crumbled, or ¼ tsp crushed red pepper flakes
- 3 strips of orange zest
- 3 strips of lemon zest

Directions:

1. Supply your smoker with wood pellets and follow the start-up procedure. Preheat the grill, with the lid closed, to 180° F.

2. Drain the olives, reserving 1 tablespoon of brine. Spread the olives in a single layer in an aluminum foil roasting pan. Place the pan on the grate and cook the olives for 30 minutes, stirring the olives or shaking the pan once or twice.

3. In a small saucepan on the stovetop over low heat, warm the olive oil. Whisk in the lemon juice and the reserved 1 tablespoon of brine. Stir in the garlic and paprika. Add the rosemary, thyme, bay leaves, chili pepper, and orange and lemon zests. Warm over low heat for 10 minutes. Remove the saucepan from the heat.

4. Transfer the olives and olive oil mixture to a pint jar. Tuck the aromatics around the sides of the jar. Let cool and then cover and refrigerate for up to 5 days. Let the olives come to room temperature before serving.

Chorizo Queso Fundido

Servings: 4-6
Cooking Time: 20 Minutes

Ingredients:

- 1 poblano chile
- 1 cup chopped queso quesadilla or queso Oaxaca
- 1 cup shredded Monterey Jack cheese
- ¼ cup milk
- 1 tablespoon all-purpose flour
- 2 (4-ounce) links Mexican chorizo sausage, casings removed
- ⅓ cup beer
- 1 tablespoon unsalted butter
- 1 small red onion, chopped
- ½ cup whole kernel corn
- 2 serrano chiles or jalapeño peppers, stemmed, seeded, and coarsely chopped
- 1 tablespoon minced garlic
- 1 tablespoon freshly squeezed lime juice
- 1 teaspoon ground cumin
- 1 teaspoon salt
- 1 teaspoon freshly ground black pepper
- 1 tablespoon chopped fresh cilantro
- 1 tablespoon chopped scallions
- Tortilla chips, for serving

Directions:

1. Supply your smoker with wood pellets and follow the start-up procedure. Preheat, with the lid closed, to 350°F.

2. On the smoker or over medium-high heat on the stove top, place the poblano directly on the grate (or burner) to char for 1 to 2 minutes, turning as needed. Remove from heat and place in a closed-up lunch-size paper bag for 2 minutes to sweat and further loosen the skin.

3. Remove the skin and coarsely chop the poblano, removing the seeds; set aside.

4. In a bowl, combine the queso quesadilla, Monterey Jack, milk, and flour; set aside.

5. On the stove top, in a cast iron skillet over medium heat, cook and crumble the chorizo for about 2 minutes.

6. Transfer the cooked chorizo to a small, grill-safe pan and place over indirect heat on the smoker.

7. Place the cast iron skillet on the preheated grill grate. Pour in the beer and simmer for a few minutes, loosening and stirring in any remaining sausage bits from the pan.

8. Add the butter to the pan, then add the cheese mixture a little at a time, stirring constantly.

9. When the cheese is smooth, stir in the onion, corn, serrano chiles, garlic, lime juice, cuvmin, salt, and pepper. Stir in the reserved chopped charred poblano.

10. Close the lid and smoke for 15 to 20 minutes to infuse the queso with smoke flavor and further cook the vegetables.

11. When the cheese is bubbly, top with the chorizo mixture and garnish with the cilantro and scallions.

12. Serve the chorizo queso fundido hot with tortilla chips.

Grilled Guacamole

Servings: 6
Cooking Time: 30 Minutes

Ingredients:

- 3 large avocados, halved and pitted
- 1 lime, halved
- ½ jalapeño, deseeded and deveined
- ½ small white or red onion, peeled
- 2 garlic cloves, peeled and skewered on a toothpick
- 1 tsp coarse salt, plus more
- 1½ tbsp reduced-fat mayo
- 2 tbsp chopped fresh cilantro
- 2 tbsp crumbled queso fresco (optional)
- tortilla chips

Directions:

1. Supply your smoker with wood pellets and follow the start-up procedure. Preheat the grill, with the lid closed, to 225° F.

2. Place the avocados, lime, jalapeño, and onion cut sides down on the grate. Use the toothpicks to balance the garlic cloves between the bars. Smoke for 30 minutes. (You want the vegetables to retain most of their rawness.)

3. Transfer everything to a cutting board. Remove the garlic cloves from the toothpick and roughly chop. Sprinkle with the salt and continue to mince the garlic until it begins to form a paste. Scrape the garlic and salt into a large bowl.

4. Scoop the avocado flesh from the peels into the bowl. Squeeze the juice of ½ lime over the avocado. Mash the avocados but leave them somewhat chunky. Finely dice the jalapeño. Dice 2 tablespoons of onion. (Reserve the remaining

onion for another use.) Add the jalapeño, onion, mayo, and cilantro to the bowl. Stir gently to combine. Taste for seasoning, adding more salt, lime juice, and jalapeño as desired.

5. Transfer the guacamole to a serving bowl. Top with the queso fresco (if using). Serve with tortilla chips.

Pigs In A Blanket

Servings: 4-6
Cooking Time: 15 Minutes

Ingredients:

- 2 Tablespoon Poppy Seeds
- 1 Tablespoon Dried Minced Onion
- 2 Teaspoon garlic, minced
- 2 Tablespoon Sesame Seeds
- 1 Teaspoon salt
- 8 Ounce Original Crescent Dough
- 1/4 Cup Dijon mustard
- 1 Large egg, beaten

Directions:

1. When ready to cook, start your smoker at 350 degrees F, and preheat with lid closed, 10 to 15 minutes.
2. Mix together poppy seeds, dried minced onion, dried minced garlic, salt and sesame seeds. Set aside.
3. Cut each triangle of crescent roll dough into thirds lengthwise, making 3 small strips from each roll.
4. Brush the dough strips lightly with Dijon mustard. Put the mini hot dogs on 1 end of the dough and roll up.
5. Arrange them, seam side down, on a greased baking pan. Brush with egg wash and sprinkle with seasoning mixture.

6. Bake in smoker until golden brown, about 12 to 15 minutes.
7. Serve with mustard or dipping sauce of your choice. Enjoy!

Simple Cream Cheese Sausage Balls

Servings: 5
Cooking Time: 30 Minutes

Ingredients:

- 1 pound ground hot sausage, uncooked
- 8 ounces cream cheese, softened
- 1 package mini filo dough shells

Directions:

1. Supply your smoker with wood pellets and follow the start-up procedure. Preheat, with the lid closed, to 350°F.
2. In a large bowl, using your hands, thoroughly mix together the sausage and cream cheese until well blended.
3. Place the filo dough shells on a rimmed perforated pizza pan or into a mini muffin tin.
4. Roll the sausage and cheese mixture into 1-inch balls and place into the filo shells.
5. Place the pizza pan or mini muffin tin on the grill, close the lid, and smoke the sausage balls for 30 minutes, or until cooked through and the sausage is no longer pink.
6. Plate and serve warm.

Deviled Eggs With Smoked Paprika

Servings: 6
Cooking Time: 30 Minutes

Ingredients:

- 6 large eggs

- 3 tbsp reduced-fat mayo, plus more
- 1 tsp Dijon or yellow mustard
- ½ tsp Spanish smoked paprika or regular paprika, plus more
- dash of hot sauce
- coarse salt
- freshly ground black pepper
- for garnishing
- small sprigs of fresh parsley, dill, tarragon, or cilantro
- chopped chives
- minced scallions
- Mustard Caviar
- sliced green or black olives
- celery leaves
- sliced radishes
- diced bell peppers
- sliced cherry tomatoes
- fresh or pickled jalapeños
- sliced or diced pickles
- slivers of sun-dried tomatoes
- bacon crumbles
- smoked salmon
- Hawaiian black salt
- Caviar

Directions:

1. Supply your smoker with wood pellets and follow the start-up procedure. Preheat the grill, with the lid closed, to 180° F.

2. On the stovetop over medium-high heat, bring a saucepan of water to a boil. (Make sure there's enough water in the saucepan to cover the eggs by 1 inch [5cm].) Use a slotted spoon to gently lower the eggs into the water. Lower the heat to maintain a simmer. Set a timer for 13 minutes.

3. Prepare an ice bath by combining ice and cold water in a large bowl. Carefully transfer the eggs to the ice bath when the timer goes off.

4. When the eggs are cool enough to handle, gently tap them all over to crack the shell. Carefully peel the eggs. Rinse under cold running water to remove any clinging bits of shell, but don't dry the eggs. (A damp surface will help the smoke adhere to the egg whites.)

5. Place the eggs on the grate and smoke until the eggs take on a light brown patina from the smoke, about 25 minutes. Transfer the eggs to a cutting board, handling them as little as possible.

6. Slice each egg in half lengthwise with a sharp knife. Wipe any yolk off the blade before slicing the next egg. Gently remove the yolks and place them in a food processor. Pulse to break up the yolks. Add the mayo, mustard, paprika, and hot sauce. Season with salt and pepper to taste. Pulse until the filling is smooth. Add additional mayo 1 teaspoon at a time if the mixture is a little dry. (It shouldn't be too loose either.)

7. Spoon the filling into each egg half or pipe it in using a small resealable plastic bag. You can also use a pastry bag fitted with a fluted tip.

8. Place the eggs on a platter and lightly dust with paprika. Accompany with one or more of the suggested garnishes.

Smoked Cashews

Servings: 6
Cooking Time: 60 Minutes

Ingredients:

- 1 pound roasted, salted cashews

Directions:

1. Supply your smoker with wood pellets and follow the start-up procedure. Preheat the grill, with the lid closed, to 120°F.

2. Pour the cashews onto a rimmed baking sheet and smoke for 1 hour, stirring once about halfway through the smoking time.

3. Remove the cashews from the grill, let cool, and store in an airtight container for as long as you can resist.

Pig Pops (sweet-hot Bacon On A Stick)

Servings: 24

Cooking Time: 30 Minutes

Ingredients:

- Nonstick cooking spray, oil, or butter, for greasing
- 2 pounds thick-cut bacon (24 slices)
- 24 metal skewers
- 1 cup packed light brown sugar
- 2 to 3 teaspoons cayenne pepper
- ½ cup maple syrup, divided

Directions:

1. Supply your smoker with wood pellets and follow the start-up procedure. Preheat, with the lid closed, to 350°F.

2. Coat a disposable aluminum foil baking sheet with cooking spray, oil, or butter.

3. Thread each bacon slice onto a metal skewer and place on the prepared baking sheet.

4. In a medium bowl, stir together the brown sugar and cayenne.

5. Baste the top sides of the bacon with ¼ cup of maple syrup.

6. Sprinkle half of the brown sugar mixture over the bacon.

7. Place the baking sheet on the grill, close the lid, and smoke for 15 to 30 minutes.

8. Using tongs, flip the bacon skewers. Baste with the remaining ¼ cup of maple syrup and top with the remaining brown sugar mixture.

9. Continue smoking with the lid closed for 10 to 15 minutes, or until crispy. You can eyeball the bacon and smoke to your desired doneness, but the actual ideal internal temperature for bacon is 155°F

10. Using tongs, carefully remove the bacon skewers from the grill. Let cool completely before handling.

Chuckwagon Beef Jerky

Servings: 6

Cooking Time: 300 Minutes

Ingredients:

- 2½lb (1.2kg) boneless top or bottom round steak, sirloin tip, flank steak, or venison
- 1 cup sugar-free dark-colored soda
- 1 cup cold brewed coffee
- ½ cup light soy sauce
- ¼ cup Worcestershire sauce
- 2 tbsp whiskey (optional)
- 2 tsp chili powder
- 1½ tsp garlic salt
- 1 tsp onion powder
- 1 tsp pink curing salt

Directions:

1. Slice the meat into ¼-inch-thick (.5cm) strips, trimming off any visible fat or gristle. (Slice against the grain for more tender jerky and with the grain for chewier jerky.) Place the meat in a large resealable plastic bag.

2. In a small bowl, whisk together the soda, coffee, soy sauce, Worcestershire sauce, whiskey

(if using), chili powder, garlic salt, onion powder, and curing salt (if using). Whisk until the salt dissolves. Pour the mixture over the meat and reseal the bag. Refrigerate for 24 to 48 hours, turning the bag several times to redistribute the brine.

3. Supply your smoker with wood pellets and follow the start-up procedure. Preheat the grill, with the lid closed, to 150° F.

4. Drain the meat and discard the brine. Place the strips of meat in a single layer on paper towels and blot any excess moisture.

5. Place the meat in a single layer on the grate and smoke for 4 to 5 hours, turning once or twice. (If you're aware of hot spots on your grate, rotate the strips so they smoke evenly.) To test for doneness, bend one or two pieces in the middle. They should be dry but still somewhat pliant. Or simply eat a piece to see if it's done to your liking.

6. For the best texture, when you remove the meat from the grill, place the still-warm jerky in a resealable plastic bag and let rest for 30 minutes. (You might see condensation form on the inside of the bag, but the moisture will be reabsorbed by the meat.) Or let the meat cool completely and then store in a resealable plastic bag or covered container. The jerky will last a few days at room temperature but will last longer (up to 2 weeks) if refrigerated.

Smoked Cheese

Servings: 4
Cooking Time: 150 Minutes

Ingredients:

• 1 (2-pound) block medium Cheddar cheese, or your favorite cheese, quartered lengthwise

Directions:

1. Supply your smoker with wood pellets and follow the start-up procedure. Preheat the grill, with the lid closed, to 90°F.

2. Place the cheese directly on the grill grate and smoke for 2 hours, 30 minutes, checking frequently to be sure it's not melting. If the cheese begins to melt, try flipping it. If that doesn't help, remove it from the grill and refrigerate for about 1 hour and then return it to the cold smoker.

3. Remove the cheese, place it in a zip-top bag, and refrigerate overnight.

4. Slice the cheese and serve with crackers, or grate it and use for making a smoked mac and cheese.

Roasted Red Pepper Dip

Servings: 8
Cooking Time: 45 Minutes

Ingredients:

• 4 red bell peppers, halved, destemmed, and deseeded
• 1 cup English walnuts, divided
• 1 small white onion, peeled and coarsely chopped
• 2 garlic cloves, peeled and smashed with a chef's knife
• ¼ cup extra virgin olive oil, plus more
• 1 tbsp balsamic vinegar or balsamic glaze
• 1 tsp honey (eliminate if using balsamic glaze)
• 1 tsp coarse salt, plus more
• 1 tsp ground cumin
• 1 tsp smoked paprika
• ½ to 1 tsp Aleppo red pepper flakes, plus more
• ¼ cup fresh white breadcrumbs (optional)
• distilled water (optional)
• assorted crudités or wedges of pita bread

Directions:

1. Supply your smoker with wood pellets and follow the start-up procedure. Preheat the grill, with the lid closed, to 400° F.

2. Place the peppers skin side down on the grate and grill until the skins blister and the flesh softens, about 30 minutes. Transfer the peppers to a bowl and cover with plastic wrap. Let cool to room temperature. Remove the skins with a paring knife or your fingers. Coarsely chop or tear the peppers.

3. Place ¾ cup of walnuts in an aluminum foil roasting pan. Place the pan on the grate and toast for 10 to 15 minutes, stirring twice. Remove the pan from the grill and let the walnuts cool.

4. Place the peppers, onion, garlic, and walnuts in a food processor fitted with the chopping blade. Pulse several times. Add the olive oil, balsamic vinegar, honey, salt, cumin, paprika, and red pepper flakes. Process until the mixture is fairly smooth. Taste for seasoning, adding more salt or red pepper flakes (if desired). (If the mixture is too loose, add breadcrumbs until the texture is to your liking. If it's too thick, add olive oil or water 1 tablespoon at a time.)

5. Transfer the dip to a serving bowl. Use the back of a spoon to make a shallow depression in the center. Top with the remaining ¼ cup of walnuts and drizzle olive oil in the depression. Serve with crudités or pita bread.

Delicious Deviled Crab Appetizer

Servings: 30

Cooking Time: 10 Minutes

Ingredients:

- Nonstick cooking spray, oil, or butter, for greasing
- 1 cup panko breadcrumbs, divided
- 1 cup canned corn, drained
- ½ cup chopped scallions, divided
- ½ red bell pepper, finely chopped
- 16 ounces jumbo lump crabmeat
- ¾ cup mayonnaise, divided
- 1 egg, beaten
- 1 teaspoon salt
- 1 teaspoon freshly ground black pepper
- 2 teaspoons cayenne pepper, divided
- Juice of 1 lemon

Directions:

1. Supply your smoker with wood pellets and follow the start-up procedure. Preheat, with the lid closed, to 425°F.

2. Spray three 12-cup mini muffin pans with cooking spray and divide ½ cup of the panko between 30 of the muffin cups, pressing into the bottoms and up the sides. (Work in batches, if necessary, depending on the number of pans you have.)

3. In a medium bowl, combine the corn, ¼ cup of scallions, the bell pepper, crabmeat, half of the mayonnaise, the egg, salt, pepper, and 1 teaspoon of cayenne pepper.

4. Gently fold in the remaining ½ cup of breadcrumbs and divide the mixture between the prepared mini muffin cups.

5. Place the pans on the grill grate, close the lid, and smoke for 10 minutes, or until golden brown.

6. In a small bowl, combine the lemon juice and the remaining mayonnaise, scallions, and cayenne pepper to make a sauce.

7. Brush the tops of the mini crab cakes with the sauce and serve hot.

Smoked Turkey Sandwich

Servings: 1
Cooking Time: 15 Minutes

Ingredients:

- 2 slices sourdough bread
- 2 tablespoons butter, at room temperature
- 2 (1-ounce) slices Swiss cheese
- 4 ounces leftover Smoked Turkey
- 1 teaspoon garlic salt

Directions:

1. Supply your smoker with wood pellets and follow the start-up procedure. Preheat the grill, with the lid closed, to 375°F.
2. Coat one side of each bread slice with 1 tablespoon of butter and sprinkle the buttered sides with garlic salt.
3. Place 1 slice of cheese on each unbuttered side of the bread, and then put the turkey on the cheese.
4. Close the sandwich, buttered sides out, and place it directly on the grill grate. Cook for 5 minutes. Flip the sandwich and cook for 5 minutes more. Remove the sandwich from the grill, cut it in half, and serve.

Sriracha & Maple Cashews

Servings: 10
Cooking Time: 60 Minutes

Ingredients:

- 2 tbsp unsalted butter
- 3 tbsp pure maple syrup
- 1 tbsp sriracha
- 1 tsp coarse salt (use only if nuts are unsalted)
- 2½ cups unsalted cashews

Directions:

1. Supply your smoker with wood pellets and follow the start-up procedure. Preheat the grill, with the lid closed, to 250° F.
2. In a small saucepan on the stovetop over low heat, melt the butter. Add the maple syrup, sriracha, and salt (if using). Stir until combined. Add the nuts and stir gently to coat thoroughly.
3. Spread the nuts in a single layer in an aluminum foil roasting pan coated with cooking spray. Place the pan on the grate and smoke the nuts until they're lightly toasted, about 1 hour, stirring once or twice.
4. Remove the pan from the grill and let the nuts cool for 15 minutes. They'll be sticky at first but will crisp up. Break them up with your fingers and store at room temperature in an airtight container, such as a lidded glass jar.

Jalapeño Poppers With Chipotle Sour Cream

Servings: 8
Cooking Time: 45 Minutes

Ingredients:

- 3 strips of thin-sliced bacon
- 12 large jalapeños, red, green, or a mix
- 8oz (225g) light cream cheese, at room temperature
- 1 cup shredded pepper Jack, Monterey Jack, or Cheddar cheese
- 1 tsp chili powder
- ½ tsp garlic salt
- smoked paprika
- for the sour cream
- 1¼ cups light sour cream
- juice of ½ lime

- ½ to 1 canned chipotle peppers in adobo sauce, finely minced, plus 1 tsp of sauce, plus more
- 1 tbsp minced fresh cilantro leaves
- ½ tsp coarse salt, plus more

Directions:

1. Supply your smoker with wood pellets and follow the start-up procedure. Preheat the grill, with the lid closed, to 375° F.

2. Line a rimmed sheet pan with aluminum foil and place a wire rack on top. Place the bacon in a single layer on the wire rack. Place the pan on the grate and grill until the bacon is crisp and golden brown, about 20 minutes. Transfer the bacon to paper towels to cool and then crumble. Set aside.

3. In a small bowl, make the chipotle sour cream by whisking together the ingredients. Add more salt, chipotle peppers, or adobe sauce to taste. Cover and refrigerate.

4. Slice the jalapeños lengthwise through their stems. Scrape out the veins and seeds with the edge of a small metal spoon.

5. In a small bowl, beat together the cream cheese, shredded cheese, chili powder, and garlic salt. Stir in the crumbled bacon. Mound the cream cheese mixture in the jalapeño halves. Line another rimmed sheet pan with aluminum foil and place a wire rack on top. Place the jalapeños filled side up in a single layer on the wire rack.

6. Place the sheet pan on the grate and roast the jalapeños until the filling has melted and the peppers have softened, about 20 to 25 minutes. (They should no longer look bright in color.) Remove the pan from the grill and let the peppers rest for 5 minutes.

7. Transfer the poppers to a platter and lightly dust with paprika. Serve with the chipotle sour cream.

Cold-smoked Cheese

Servings: 6
Cooking Time: 180 Minutes

Ingredients:

- 2lb (1kg) well-chilled hard or semi-hard cheese, such as:
- Edam
- Gouda
- Cheddar
- Monterey Jack
- pepper Jack
- goat cheese
- fresh mozzarella
- Muenster
- aged Parmigiano-Reggiano
- Gruyère
- blue cheese

Directions:

1. Unwrap the cheese and remove any protective wax or coating. Cut into 4-ounce (110g) portions to increase the surface area.

2. If possible, move your smoker to a shady area. Place 1 resealable plastic bag filled with ice on top of the drip pan. This is especially important on a warm day because you want to keep the interior temperature of the grill between 70 and 90°F (21 and 32°C) or below.

3. Place a grill mat on one side of the grate. Place the cheese on the mat and allow space between each piece.

4. Fill your smoking tube or pellet maze (see Cast Iron Skillets and Grill Pans) with pellets or sawdust and light according to the manufacturer's

instructions. Place the smoking tube on the grate near—but not on—the grill mat. When the tube is smoking consistently, close the grill lid.

5. Smoke the cheese for 1 to 3 hours, replacing the pellets or sawdust and ice if necessary. Monitor the temperature and make sure the cheese isn't beginning to melt. Carefully lift the mat with the cheese to a rimmed baking sheet and let the cheese cool completely before handling.

6. Package the smoked cheese in cheese storage paper or bags or vacuum-seal the cheese, labeling each. (While you can wrap the cheese tightly in plastic wrap, the cheese will spoil faster.) Let the cheese rest for at least 2 to 3 days before eating. It will be even better after 2 weeks.

Wild West Wings

Servings: 4

Cooking Time: 60 Minutes

Ingredients:

- 2 pounds chicken wings
- 2 tablespoons extra-virgin olive oil
- 2 packages ranch dressing mix (such as Hidden Valley brand)
- ¼ cup prepared ranch dressing (optional)

Directions:

1. Supply your smoker with wood pellets and follow the start-up procedure. Preheat, with the lid closed, to 350°F.

2. Place the chicken wings in a large bowl and toss with the olive oil and ranch dressing mix.

3. Arrange the wings directly on the grill, or line the grill with aluminum foil for easy cleanup, close the lid, and smoke for 25 minutes.

4. Flip and smoke for 20 to 35 minutes more, or until a meat thermometer inserted in the thickest part of the wings reads 165°F and the wings are crispy. (Note: The wings will likely be done after 45 minutes, but an extra 10 to 15 minutes makes them crispy without drying the meat.)

5. Serve warm with ranch dressing (if using).

Chicken Egg Rolls With Buffalo Sauce

Servings: 4

Cooking Time: 75 Minutes

Ingredients:

- 1/4 Cup Bleu Cheese, Crumbled
- 1/4 Cup Buffalo Sauce
- 1 Lb Chicken Breasts - Boneless, Skinless
- 4 Oz Cream Cheese, Softened
- 8 Egg Roll Wrappers
- 1/2 Jalapeno Pepper, Minced
- Pinch Sweet Heat Rub
- 1/4 Red Bell Pepper, Chopped
- 4 Scallion, Sliced Thin
- 1/4 Cup Sour Cream
- 2 Cups Vegetable Oil

Directions:

1. Supply your smoker with wood pellets and follow the start-up procedure. Preheat the grill, with the lid open, to 200° F. If using a gas or charcoal grill, set it up for low, indirect heat.

2. Season chicken breasts with Sweet Heat Rub, then place on the grill. Smoke for 1 hour, then remove from the grill, cool, shred, and set aside.

3. Prepare the filling: In a mixing bowl, use a hand mixer to blend cream cheese, bleu cheese, Buffalo sauce and sour cream.

4. Fold in scallions, jalapeño, red bell pepper, and shredded chicken.

5. Prepare egg rolls: Lay an egg roll wrapper on a flat surface and add 3 tablespoons of filling to the middle.

6. Fold the bottom of the wrapper over the top of the filling, then fold over each side. Brush the top point of the wrapper with warm water, then roll the wrapper tight. Transfer to a tray while filling the remaining wrappers.

7. Increase the temperature of the grill to 425°F, then set a cast iron Dutch oven on the grill. Add vegetable oil and heat for 5 minutes.

8. Place 3 egg rolls in heated oil and fry until golden, 1 to 2 minutes per side.

9. Transfer to a wire rack to cool, then fry the remaining egg rolls, in batches.

10. Cool egg rolls for 2 minutes, then slice in half and serve warm with celery sticks and extra Buffalo sauce for dipping.

Peanut Butter Chicken Wings

Servings: 4

Cooking Time: 35 Minutes

Ingredients:

- 1 Tsp Black Peppercorns, Ground
- 2 Tbsp Brown Sugar
- 4 Lbs Chicken Wings, Trimmed And Patted Dry
- 2 Tbsp Honey
- 1/4 Cup Peanut Butter
- 10 Oz Peanuts, Whole
- 2 Tsp Sweet Rib Rub
- 1/2 Red Onion, Minced
- 1/2 Cup Strawberry Preserves
- 1 Tbsp Thai Chili Sauce
- 1/4 Cup Worcestershire Sauce

Directions:

1. Place chicken wings in a 9 x13 glass baking dish. Pour mixture over chicken, cover with plastic wrap, and refrigerate for 2 hours.

2. Supply your smoker with wood pellets and follow the start-up procedure. Preheat the grill, with the lid open, to 400° F. Preheat griddle to medium-low flame. If using a gas or charcoal grill, set it to medium-high heat.

3. Place wings directly on grill grate, over indirect heat, and cook for 20 to 25 minutes, rotating wings every 5 minutes.

4. Meanwhile, place shelled peanuts on the griddle, turning occasionally with a metal spatula for 5 to 7 minutes, to lightly roast. Remove from the griddle and set aside to cool.

5. Remove wings from grill and allow to rest for 5 minutes. While wings are resting, shell the peanuts, and transfer to a resealable plastic bag. Use a rolling pin to crush the peanuts, then scatter peanuts on top of the chicken wings. Serve warm.

Grilled Greek Chicken With Garlic & Lemon

Servings: 4

Cooking Time: 60 Minutes

Ingredients:

- 2 Whole Roasting Chicken, 3.5-4lbs, each cut into 8 pieces
- 2 Whole lemons, quartered
- Cup extra-virgin olive oil
- 4 Clove garlic, minced
- 1 1/2 Tablespoon Oregano, fresh
- 1 As Needed Chicken Rub
- 1 Cup Broth, chicken

Directions:

1. Arrange the chicken pieces in a single layer in a large roasting pan. Squeeze the juice from each piece of lemon over the chicken, catching any seeds in your fingers. Tuck the lemon rinds in with the chicken. Drizzle the olive oil over all.

2. Sprinkle the garlic over the chicken. Dust the chicken with the fresh oregano, and season it generously with the Traeger Chicken rub, or salt and black pepper. Pour the chicken broth into the pan.

3. Supply your smoker with wood pellets and follow the start-up procedure. Preheat the grill, with the lid closed, to 350° F.

4. Roast the chicken for an hour, or until the juices run clear or the internal temperature reaches 165°F on an instant-read meat thermometer. Grill: 350 °F Probe: 165 °F

5. Transfer to a platter or plates and spoon some of the juices on top. Let rest 3 minutes before serving. Enjoy!

Applewood-smoked Whole Turkey

Servings: 6-8
Cooking Time: 300 Minutes

Ingredients:
- 1 (10- to 12-pound) turkey, giblets removed
- Extra-virgin olive oil, for rubbing
- ¼ cup poultry seasoning
- 8 tablespoons (1 stick) unsalted butter, melted
- ½ cup apple juice
- 2 teaspoons dried sage
- 2 teaspoons dried thyme

Directions:
1. Supply your smoker with wood pellets and follow the start-up procedure. Preheat, with the lid closed, to 250°F.
2. Rub the turkey with oil and season with the poultry seasoning inside and out, getting under the skin.
3. In a bowl, combine the melted butter, apple juice, sage, and thyme to use for basting.
4. Put the turkey in a roasting pan, place on the grill, close the lid, and grill for 5 to 6 hours, basting every hour, until the skin is brown and crispy, or until a meat thermometer inserted in the thickest part of the thigh reads 165°F.
5. Let the bird rest for 15 to 20 minutes before carving.

Smoked Chicken With Apricot Bbq Glaze

Servings: 4
Cooking Time: 60 Minutes

Ingredients:
- 2 Whole Chickens, halved
- 4 Tablespoon Chicken Rub
- 1 Cup Apricot BBQ Sauce

Directions:
1. Supply your smoker with wood pellets and follow the start-up procedure. Preheat the grill, with the lid closed, to 375° F.
2. Season chicken with Chicken Rub and place on grill meat side up. Cook 1 hour or until internal temperature has reached 160°F in the breast and 175°F in the leg. Grill: 375 °F Probe: 160 °F
3. Baste each chicken half with a bit of the Apricot BBQ glaze and return to grill for 10 minutes. Grill: 375 °F
4. Remove chicken from the grill and allow to rest 5-10 minutes. Portion each half by removing the leg and cutting each breast in half leaving you with four legs and 8 breast pieces. Serve with your favorite vegetables or sides. Enjoy!

Yucatán-spiced Chicken Thighs

Servings: 4
Cooking Time: 40 Minutes

Ingredients:
- 8 skin-on, bone-in chicken thighs, about 2½lb (1.2kg) total
- for the marinade
- 2oz (55g) achiote paste
- ¼ cup hot distilled water
- ¼ cup freshly squeezed orange juice

- 2 tbsp freshly squeezed lime juice
- 2 tbsp apple cider vinegar or distilled white vinegar
- 2 tbsp vegetable oil or extra virgin olive oil
- 2 garlic cloves, peeled and minced
- 1 tsp kosher salt, plus more
- 1 tsp dried Mexican oregano
- ½ tsp ground cumin
- ¼ tsp ground cinnamon

Directions:

1. In a small bowl, make the marinade by using a fork to crumble the achiote paste. Add the hot water and mash the paste with the fork until blended. Whisk in the orange juice, lime juice, vinegar, oil, garlic, salt, oregano, cumin, and cinnamon.

2. Place the chicken thighs in a resealable plastic bag. Pour the marinade over the chicken, turning and massaging the bag to thoroughly coat the chicken. Refrigerate for 2 hours.

3. Supply your smoker with wood pellets and follow the start-up procedure. Preheat the grill, with the lid closed, to 400° F.

4. Remove the chicken thighs from the marinade and let any excess drip off. (Discard the marinade.) Place the chicken thighs skin side down on the grate at an angle to the bars. Grill for 20 minutes and then turn. Continue to grill until the internal temperature in the thighs reaches 165°F (74°C), about 20 minutes more.

5. Transfer the thighs to a platter and serve immediately.

Easy Bbq Chicken Wings

Servings: 4

Cooking Time: 40 Minutes

Ingredients:

- 1 Pack Chicken Wings
- Extra Virgin Olive Oil
- Champion Chicken Seasoning

Directions:

1. Supply your smoker with wood pellets and follow the start-up procedure. Preheat the grill, with the lid closed, to 350° F.

2. Blot the defrosted chicken wings dry with paper towels.

3. Brush oil onto each side of the wings and sprinkle with seasoning.

4. Grill at 350° for 40 minutes or until wings are crispy. Flip halfway through. Serve hot.

Smoked Apple Chicken Leg Quarters

Servings: 8

Cooking Time: 120 Minutes

Ingredients:

- 8 leg quarters
- 1 bottle marinade
- Pork & chicken rub
- 1 cup of apple juice or water

Directions:

1. Rinse chicken and pat dry.

2. Marinade chicken in the fridge for at least 30 minutes or overnight (preferred).

3. Once the chicken is marinated, sprinkle both sides with the rub.

4. Supply your smoker with wood pellets and follow the start-up procedure. Preheat the grill, with the lid closed, to 225° F.

5. Place a small stainless steel pot of apple juice or water in the inside corner to help keep moist.

6. Place chicken on your grill, skin side up, with lid closed.

7. Smoke for 2 hours or until the internal temperature in the thickest part of a thigh is 165 °F.

8. Remove chicken from the grill and let it rest for 5 minutes before serving. Enjoy!

Green Chile Chicken Enchiladas

Servings: 6
Cooking Time: 45 Minutes

Ingredients:
- 2 Cups Chicken, Shredded
- 1 (12 Oz) Package Colby Jack Cheese, Shredded
- 1 Enchilada Sauce, Can
- 1 Can Green Chile, Drained
- 1 Onion, Diced
- 1 Tablespoon Sweet Rib Rub
- 1 Cup Sour Cream
- 1 Package Flour Tortilla

Directions:
1. Supply your smoker with wood pellets and follow the start-up procedure. Preheat the grill, with the lid open, to 300° F.

2. In a bowl, mix - the chicken, green chiles, Sweet Heat seasoning, sour cream, diced onion, and half the bag of shredded cheese.

3. Place a large spoonful of the chicken mixture in the center of a tortilla and roll it up. Repeat with the remaining tortillas, then place in the baking pan, and pour the enchilada sauce over the tortilla pans. Top with the remainder of the shredded cheese.

4. Wrap the top of the pan tightly in aluminum foil and grill for 45 minutes or until the enchilada sauce is bubbly. Remove from the grill and serve.

Delicious Asian Bbq Wings

Servings: 6
Cooking Time: 60 Minutes

Ingredients:
- 2 Lbs Chicken, Wing
- 1 Tsp Garlic, Minced
- 1 Tsp Ginger, Fresh
- 1 Tsp Chopped Green Onion
- 1/2 Cup Hoisin Sauce
- 1 Tsp Honey
- 2 Tsp Rice Vinegar
- 2 Tsp Sesame Oil
- 1 Tsp Sesame Seeds
- 1 Tsp Soy Sauce
- 1 Cup Water, Boiling

Directions:
1. Add all ingredients except wings and sesame seeds to a mixing bowl and whisk to incorporate. Add wings to a resealable plastic bag and pour marinade over. Allow marinating for at least 2 hours up to overnight. Remove wings from bag, reserving marinade.

2. Supply your smoker with wood pellets and follow the start-up procedure. Preheat the grill, with the lid closed, to 300° F. Place wings in a grilling basket and cook for 1 hour or until they reach an internal temperature of 165°F.

3. While wings are cooking, pour reserved marinade into a small saucepan and add rice wine vinegar. Over high heat, bring to a boil while whisking often, and reduce by 1/3, or about 10 minutes. Set aside.

4. Brush wings with reduced sauce and allow to cook for 5-10 more minutes or until glaze has set. Remove from smoker, sprinkle with sesame seeds, allow to rest for 5 minutes, and serve.

Smoked Chicken Vermicelli Noodles

Servings: 4 – 6
Cooking Time: 120 Minutes

Ingredients:

- 2 Cup Broccoli
- ¼ Cup Chicken Stock
- 6 - 8 Chicken Thighs, Boneless, Skinless
- 1 Tbsp Chili Flakes
- 1 Tsp Cornstarch
- 4, Chopped Garlic Cloves
- 3 Tbsp Hoisin Sauce, Divided
- Knob Of Fresh Ginger, Grated
- 1, Thin Red Bell Peppers, Sliced
- 1 Tbsp Rice Wine Vinegar
- 8 Scallions, Sliced
- 1 ½ Tbsp Sesame Oil, Divided
- 1 Tbsp, Toasted Sesame Seeds
- 3.5 Oz Shitake Mushrooms, Sliced Thin
- 8 Oz Snow Peas
- 3 Tbsp Soy Sauce
- 2 Tbsp Sweet Chili Sauce
- 3 Tbsp Vegetable Oil
- 1 Lb Vermicelli Noodles, Or Linguini, Cooked And Drained

Directions:

1. In a large bowl, whisk together rice wine vinegar, 1 tablespoon of Hoisin sauce, and 1 tablespoon of sesame oil. Toss chicken to coat and allow to marinate for 1 hour.

2. Supply your smoker with wood pellets and follow the start-up procedure. Preheat the grill, with the lid open, to 225° F. If using a gas or charcoal grill, set it for low, indirect heat. Place chicken directly on the grill grate and smoke for 1 ½ to 2 hours, or until the internal temperature reaches 165° F. Remove it from the smoker, cover with foil, and rest for 10 minutes, then slice thin and set aside.

3. In a glass measuring cup whisk together 2 tablespoons of Hoisin sauce, soy sauce, sweet chili sauce, chicken stock, ½ tablespoon of sesame oil, and cornstarch. Set aside.

4. Preheat griddle to medium flame, then add oil. Working quickly, sauté ginger and garlic for 15 seconds, then add bell pepper and mushrooms and continue cooking for another minute, then add in snow peas and slaw. Toss in cooked pasta, chicken, scallions, and pour sauce over. Cook for one minute until sauce thickens and is well incorporated.

5. Transfer to platter and serve hot. Sprinkle with chili flakes and sesame seeds, if desired.

Cheese Buffalo Chicken Wings

Servings: 4-6
Cooking Time: 25 Minutes

Ingredients:

- Bleu Cheese Dip
- ⅔ Cup Buffalo Sauce
- Celery
- 2 Lbs. Chicken Wings
- ½ Cup Sweet Heat Rub

Directions:

1. Supply your smoker with wood pellets and follow the start-up procedure. Preheat the grill, with the lid open, to 450° F. If using a gas or charcoal grill, set heat to high heat.

2. Rub wings generously with Sweet Heat Rub and transfer to wing rack.

3. Place rack on grill and cook for 20 minutes, rotating after 10 minutes.

4. Baste with sauce, then cover and grill an additional 5 to 7 minutes. Note: your cooking time will vary depending on the size of the wings. When done, wings should have an internal temperature of 165°F.

5. Remove wings from grill and transfer to a baking sheet and let rest for about 5 minutes.

6. Transfer wings to a large bowl and coat with the Buffalo Sauce. Shake the bowl around gently to combine or use a spatula to ensure every wing is coated.

7. Serve hot with extra sauce, celery, and bleu cheese dip.

Savory Jerk Chicken Wings

Servings: 4
Cooking Time: 20 Minutes

Ingredients:
- 1 Tsp Allspice, Ground
- 3 Lbs Chicken Wings, Split
- 1/2 Tsp Cinnamon, Ground
- 4 Garlic Cloves, Smashed
- 2 Tsp Ginger, Grated
- 1 Habanero Pepper, Chopped
- 2 Tbsp Honey
- 2 Tbsp Lemon Juice
- 1/3 Cup Lime Juice
- 1/2 Tsp Nutmeg, Ground
- 1/2 Cup Olive Oil
- 1/4 Cup Poblano Pepper, Chopped
- 1 Tbsp Tamari
- 2 Tsp Thyme, Dried
- 1/2 Cup Yellow Onion, Chopped

Directions:
1. Add chicken to a large resealable plastic bag.
2. In the bowl of a food processor, add the garlic, onion, ginger, peppers, tamari, honey, lime juice, lemon juice, thyme, allspice, cinnamon, nutmeg, and oil. Process on low for 1 minute, then transfer marinade to the bag. Seal the bag and place in the refrigerator for at least 2 hours, up to overnight.

3. Supply your smoker with wood pellets and follow the start-up procedure. Preheat the grill, with the lid open, to 425° F. If using a gas or charcoal grill, set it up for medium-high heat.

4. Remove wings from the marinade, and discard remaining marinade. Place wings on the grill and cook for 15 to 20 minutes, flipping every 5 minutes, until an internal temperature of 165 F is reached.

5. Remove wings from the grill and serve warm.

Smoked Whole Chicken

Servings: 6-8
Cooking Time: 240 Minutes

Ingredients:
- 1 whole chicken
- 2 cups Tea Injectable (using Not-Just-for-Pork Rub)
- 2 tablespoons olive oil
- 1 batch Chicken Rub
- 2 tablespoons butter, melted

Directions:
1. Supply your smoker with wood pellets and follow the start-up procedure. Preheat the grill, with the lid closed, to 180°F.

2. Inject the chicken throughout with the tea injectable.

3. Coat the chicken all over with olive oil and season it with the rub. Using your hands, work the rub into the meat.

4. Place the chicken directly on the grill grate and smoke for 3 hours.

5. Baste the chicken with the butter and increase the grill's temperature to 375°F. Continue to cook the chicken until its internal temperature reaches 170°F.

6. Remove the chicken from the grill and let it rest for 10 minutes, before carving and serving.

Bacon-wrapped Chicken Breasts

Servings: 4 - 6

Cooking Time: 270 Minutes

Ingredients:

- 5 Oz Frozen Spinach, Thawed, Strained
- 8 Bacon Slices
- 1 Tbsp Butter
- 4 Chicken Breasts, Boneless, Skinless, Butterflied
- 2 Garlic Clove, Minced
- 1 Cup Italian Cheese Blend, Shredded
- 8 Oz Mushrooms, Sliced Thin
- 1 Tbsp Olive Oil
- 1 Tbsp Hickory Bacon Rub
- 1 Yellow Onion, Chopped

Directions:

1. Supply your smoker with wood pellets and follow the start-up procedure. Preheat the grill, with the lid open, to 375° F. If using a gas or charcoal grill, set heat to medium heat. For all other grills, preheat cast iron skillet on grill grates.

2. Heat olive oil and butter on griddle, then add mushrooms and cook for about 3 minutes, stirring frequently. Add chopped onion and garlic and cook for 2 minutes. Add spinach and sauté another minute, then transfer vegetables to a heat-safe bowl to cool slightly.

3. Season the butterflied chicken breasts with Hickory Bacon, coating both sides. Sprinkle half of cheese over each butterflied chicken breast, followed by the sautéed vegetables, and the remaining half of the cheese.

4. On a metal sheet tray, lay out two bacon slices. Gently fold chicken breast halves together and place on top of bacon slices, then wrap tightly with bacon. To secure, tuck ends of bacon underneath, or insert a toothpick to hold it together. Repeat with remaining breasts.

5. Arrange the chicken breasts, bacon seam down, directly on the grill grate and grill, turning once or twice, until the bacon is crisp and golden brown, about 25 to 30 minutes, or until internal temperature reaches 165°F.

6. Remove from grill, allow to rest for 5 minutes, remove any toothpicks, then serve hot.

Delicious Smoked Turketta

Servings: 6

Cooking Time: 180 Minutes

Ingredients:

- 1 Shady Brook Farms® Turketta

Directions:

1. Supply your smoker with wood pellets and follow the start-up procedure. Preheat the grill, with the lid closed, to 250° F. If using a gas or charcoal grill, set it up for low, indirect heat.

2. Place the Turketta directly on the grill grate and smoke for 2½ to 3 hours, or until an internal temperature of 165°F is reached.

Chicken On A Throne

Servings: 6.

Cooking Time: 75 Minutes

Ingredients:

- 1 can of low-carb beer or sugar-free dark-colored soda, about 12oz (350ml)
- 1 whole chicken, about 4lb (1.8kg)

- 3 tbsp barbecue rub, plus more

Directions:

1. Supply your smoker with wood pellets and follow the start-up procedure. Preheat the grill, with the lid closed, to 350° F.

2. Pour half the contents of the can into a glass for drinking. Set the half-full can aside.

3. Blot any juices off the chicken with paper towels. Sprinkle 2 teaspoons of the rub in the body and neck cavities. Sprinkle the remaining rub evenly on the outside. Tuck the wing tips behind the bird's back.

4. Carefully lower the chicken (body cavity side down) over the can. Place the chicken upright on its can on the grate. (For stability, pull the legs forward and rest them on the grate to essentially form a tripod.) Roast the chicken until the internal temperature in the thickest part of a thigh reaches 165°F (74°C), about 1 hour. (Check on your bird periodically to make sure it hasn't tipped over.) If it hasn't yet reached that temperature, continue cooking for about 15 minutes more.

5. Use heavy-duty insulated rubber gloves and tongs to carefully transfer the chicken to the kitchen. Let rest 5 minutes and then carefully ease the chicken off the can. Discard the can and its steaming liquid, being careful not to burn yourself. Carve the chicken and serve.

Cajun Brined Maple Smoked Turkey Breast

Servings: 4
Cooking Time: 180 Minutes

Ingredients:

- 1 Gallon water
- 3/4 Cup canning and pickling salt
- 3 Tablespoon minced garlic
- 3 Tablespoon dark brown sugar
- 2 Tablespoon Worcestershire sauce
- 2 Tablespoon Cajun seasoning
- 1 (5-6 lb) bone-in turkey breast
- 3 Tablespoon extra-virgin olive oil
- 2 Tablespoon Cajun seasoning

Directions:

1. In a large food safe container or bucket, combine all of the ingredients for the brine with 1 gallon water. Stir until the salt is dissolved.

2. Place the turkey breast in the brine and weigh it down to ensure it is fully submerged. Cover and brine in a refrigerator for 1 to 2 days.

3. Remove the turkey breast from the brine and pat dry. Drizzle with the olive oil using your hands to cover all areas of the bird. Season liberally with Cajun seasoning. Probe: 165 °F

4. Supply your smoker with wood pellets and follow the start-up procedure. Preheat the grill, with the lid closed, to 225° F.

5. Place the turkey breast directly on the grill grate, close the lid and cook for 3 hours. After 3 hours, increase the temperature to 425°F and continue to cook for another 30 minutes or until the internal temperature reads 165°F when a thermometer is inserted into the thickest part of the breast. Grill: 225 °F Probe: 165 °F

6. Remove the turkey breast from the grill and allow to rest for at least 15 minutes before slicing. Slice and serve. Enjoy!

Grilled Cheesy Chicken

Servings: 4
Cooking Time: 45 Minutes

Ingredients:

- 4 Aged Chedder Cheese, Sliced
- 32 Oz Chicken Broth
- 1 Tsp Extra-Virgin Olive Oil
- Sweet Heat Rub And Grill
- 4 Plump Chicken, Boneless/Skinless

Directions:

1. Supply your smoker with wood pellets and follow the start-up procedure. Preheat the grill, with the lid open, to 350° F.

2. Remove the chicken from the brine. Pat the breasts dry and lightly brush olive oil on both sides of the chicken. Take your knife and slice diagonally across the top of each breast. Sprinkle a lit amount of   Sweet Heat Rub and Grill on each side.

3. Barbecue your chicken breasts for 30 minutes. Next, place a slice of cheddar cheese on top of each breast.

4. Heat for another 5-10 minutes or until the cheese has fully melted into the incisions you made earlier. Remove and serve for a tender chicken breast with a spicy kick and hot cheesy center. You'll receive too much credit for a recipe this easy.

Spiced Bbq Turkey

Servings: 8
Cooking Time: 120 Minutes

Ingredients:

- 1 Bay Leaf
- 1/2 Tsp Black Peppercorns, Ground
- Pinch Chili Flakes
- 4 Garlic Cloves, Peeled And Smashed
- 1/4 Cup Honey
- 3/4 Cup Honey Chipotle Bbq Sauce
- 1 Honeysuckle White® Turkey, Thawed
- 1 Tsp Kosher Salt
- 1/4 Cup Olive Oil
- 3 Thyme Sprigs
- 1 Cup Turkey Stock
- 3 Cups Water
- 2 Tbsp Worcestershire Sauce

Directions:

1. Rinse Honeysuckle White® turkey thoroughly under cold water, then blot dry with paper towels. Place on a greased rack of a roasting pan. Set aside.

2. Prepare the injection solution: in a saucepot, whisk together the turkey stock, honey, olive oil, smashed garlic, Worcestershire sauce, salt, pepper, and chili flakes. Add in the thyme sprigs and bay leaf. Bring mixture to a boil, then simmer for 5 minutes. Remove from heat, cool for 30 minutes, then strain.

3. Using an injection needle, inject the solution throughout the turkey. Rub 1 tablespoon of solution over the top of the turkey. Add water to the bottom of the roasting pan. Set aside.

4. Supply your smoker with wood pellets and follow the start-up procedure. Preheat the grill, with the lid closed, to 450° F. If using a gas or charcoal grill, set it up for high heat.

5. Transfer the turkey to the grill and roast for 100 to 120 minutes, until an internal temperature of 165° F is reached, rotating every 30 minutes. Tent with foil after 30 minutes, then brush all over with BBQ sauce during the final 10 minutes of roasting time.

6. Remove from the grill, and allow the turkey to rest for 30 minutes, then carve and serve warm.

Beer Chicken

Servings: 4

Cooking Time: 75 Minutes

Ingredients:

- 1 Beer, Can
- 1 Chicken, Whole
- Lemon Pepper Garlic Seasoning

Directions:

1. Supply your smoker with wood pellets and follow the start-up procedure. Preheat the grill, with the lid open, to 400° F.

2. Season the chicken all over with spices. Open the can of your favorite pop/beer and place the opening of the chicken over the can. Make sure that the chicken can stand upright without falling over. Place on your Grill and barbecue until the internal temperature reaching 165 degrees F (about an hour).

3. Remove from grill, slice and serve hot.

Savory Smoked Turkey Legs

Servings: 4

Cooking Time: 150 Minutes

Ingredients:

- 1 Cup Chicken Stock
- 2 Tbsp Blackened Sriracha Rub
- 4 Turkey Legs (Drumsticks)

Directions:

1. Fire up your pellet grill on SMOKE mode. With the lid open, let it run for 10 minutes.

2. Supply your smoker with wood pellets and follow the start-up procedure. Preheat the grill, with the lid closed, to 225° F. If using a gas or charcoal grill, set it up for low, indirect heat.

3. Combine turkey stock with 2 teaspoons of Blackened Sriracha Rub.

4. Place turkey legs on a sheet tray, then inject each with seasoned stock. Season the outside of the legs with remaining Blackened Sriracha.

5. Place turkey legs directly on the grate of the smoking cabinet, and cook for 1 ½ hours.

6. Increase temperature to 325°F, then transfer turkey legs to the bottom grill and cook for another 45 to 60 minutes, until the internal temperature reaches 170°F.

7. Remove turkey from the grill, allow to rest for 10 minutes, then serve warm.

Bacon Wrapped Turkey Legs

Servings: 8

Cooking Time: 180 Minutes

Ingredients:

- 1 Gallon water
- 1/4 Cup Rub
- 3 Cup Morton Tender Quick Home Meat Cure
- 1/2 Cup brown sugar
- 6 Whole black peppercorns
- 2 Whole bay leaves
- 8 (1-1/2 lb each) turkey legs
- 8 Slices bacon

Directions:

1. Plan ahead, these turkey legs brine overnight. In a large stockpot, combine one gallon of water, Traeger Rub, curing salt, brown sugar, peppercorns and bay leaves.

2. Bring to a boil over high heat to dissolve the salt and sugar granules. Take off of the heat and add in 1/2 gallon of water and ice. Make sure the brine is at least to room temperature, if not colder. (You may need to refrigerate the brine for an hour or so.)

3. Add the turkey legs making sure they are completely submerged in the brine.

4. After 24 hours, drain the turkey legs and discard the brine. Rinse the brine off the legs with cold water, then dry thoroughly with paper towels.

5. Supply your smoker with wood pellets and follow the start-up procedure. Preheat the grill, with the lid closed, to 250° F.

6. Lay the turkey legs directly on the grill grate.

7. After 2-1/2 hours, wrap a piece of bacon around each leg and finish cooking them for the last 30 to 40 minutes. Grill: 250 °F

8. The total cooking time for the legs will be 3 hours, or until the internal temperature reaches 165°F on an instant-read meat thermometer. Serve and enjoy! Grill: 250 °F Probe: 165 °F

Jalapeño- & Cheese-stuffed Chicken

Servings: 4
Cooking Time: 30 Minutes

Ingredients:

- 4 boneless, skinless chicken breasts, each about 6 to 8oz (170 to 225g)
- 8 strips of thin-sliced bacon
- for the filling
- 4oz (110g) light cream cheese, at room temperature
- ⅓ cup shredded pepper Jack or Cheddar cheese
- 2 jalapeños, destemmed, deseeded, and minced
- 2 tbsp reduced-fat mayo
- 1 tsp chili powder
- ½ tsp coarse salt

Directions:

1. Supply your smoker with wood pellets and follow the start-up procedure. Preheat the grill, with the lid closed, to 375° F.

2. In a large bowl, make the filling by combining the ingredients. Mix well.

3. Use a sharp, thin-bladed knife to cut a deep pocket in the side of each chicken breast, angling the knife toward the opposite side. (Don't cut all the way through.) Spoon ¼ of the cheese filling into the pocket of each breast and gently press the edges of the pocket together to enclose. Wrap 2 slices of bacon in a spiral pattern around each breast.

4. Place the chicken on the grate at an angle to the bars. Grill until the chicken is cooked through, the filling melts, and the bacon is golden brown, about 25 to 30 minutes.

5. Transfer the pockets to a platter. Let rest for 2 minutes before serving.

Baked Garlic Parmesan Wings

Servings: 4
Cooking Time: 40 Minutes

Ingredients:

- 3 1/2 Tablespoon Chicken Rub
- 5 Pound chicken wings
- 1 Cup butter
- 10 Clove garlic, minced
- 1/2 Cup unsalted butter
- 10 Clove garlic, finely diced
- 1 Cup shredded Parmesan cheese
- 3 Tablespoon chopped parsley

Directions:

1. Supply your smoker with wood pellets and follow the start-up procedure. Preheat the grill, with the lid closed, to 450° F.

2. In a large bowl, toss the wings with the Traeger Chicken Rub.

3. Place wings directly on the grill grate and cook for 20 minutes. Flip wings and cook for an additional 20 minutes. Grill: 450 ˚F

4. Check the internal temperature of the wings, finished desired temperature is 165˚F to 180˚F. Grill: 450 ˚F Probe: 165 ˚F

5. To make the Garlic Sauce: While the chicken is cooking, combine butter, garlic and remaining rub in a medium sized saucepan and cook over medium heat on a stove top. Cook sauce for 8 to 10 minutes, stirring occasionally.

6. When wings are finished cooking, remove from grill and place in a large bowl. Toss wings with the garlic sauce, Parmesan cheese and parsley. Enjoy!

Mini Turducken Roulade

Servings: 6
Cooking Time: 120 Minutes

Ingredients:

- 1 (16-ounce) boneless turkey breast
- 1 (8-to 10-ounce) boneless duck breast
- 1 (8-ounce) boneless, skinless chicken breast
- Salt
- Freshly ground black pepper
- 2 cups Italian dressing
- 2 tablespoons Cajun seasoning
- 1 cup prepared seasoned stuffing mix
- 8 slices bacon
- Butcher's string

Directions:

1. Butterfly the turkey, duck, and chicken breasts, cover with plastic wrap and, using a mallet, flatten each ½ inch thick.

2. Season all the meat on both sides with a little salt and pepper.

3. In a medium bowl, combine the Italian dressing and Cajun seasoning. Spread one-fourth of the mixture on top of the flattened turkey breast.

4. Place the duck breast on top of the turkey, spread it with one-fourth of the dressing mixture, and top with the stuffing mix.

5. Place the chicken breast on top of the duck and spread with one-fourth of the dressing mixture.

6. Supply your smoker with wood pellets and follow the start-up procedure. Preheat, with the lid closed, to 275°F.

7. Tightly roll up the stack, tie with butcher's string, and slather the whole thing with the remaining dressing mixture.

8. Wrap the bacon slices around the turducken and secure with toothpicks, or try making a bacon weave (see the technique for this in the Jalapeño-Bacon Pork Tenderloin recipe).

9. Place the turducken roulade in a roasting pan. Transfer to the grill, close the lid, and roast for 2 hours, or until a meat thermometer inserted in the turducken reads 165°F. Tent with aluminum foil in the last 30 minutes, if necessary, to keep from overbrowning.

10. Let the turducken rest for 15 to 20 minutes before carving. Serve warm.

Chicken Nachos

Servings: 6-8
Cooking Time: 10 Minutes

Ingredients:

- 1 Can Black Beans, Rinsed And Drained
- 1 Cup Cheddar Cheese, Shredded
- 2 Cups Chicken, Diced

- (If Desired) Cilantro
- 1 Can Corn Kernels, Drained
- (If Desired) Pickled Jalapeno Peppers
- 1/2 Tablespoon Champion Chicken Seasoning
- 1/2 Red Onion, Diced
- 1/2 Cup Salsa
- 1/4 Cup Sour Cream

Directions:

1. On a large sheet pan, spread out half the tortilla chips, then cover with half the shredded cheese and one cup of chicken. Sprinkle with half of Champion Chicken seasoning. Top with the rest of the tortilla chips, cheese, chicken and remaining seasoning.

2. Supply your smoker with wood pellets and follow the start-up procedure. Preheat the grill, with the lid closed, to 350° F. Grill for 5-7 minutes, or until the cheese is melted and bubbly and everything is warmed all the way through. Remove the pan from the grill.

3. Top the nachos with the black beans, corn, diced red onion, sour cream, cilantro and pickled jalapenos. Serve and enjoy!

Lemon & Herb Chicken

Servings: 3-4
Cooking Time: 75 Minutes

Ingredients:

- 1 roaster chicken, about 4lb (1.8kg), preferably organic
- 1 large sweet onion, peeled and sliced lengthwise into 8 wedges
- ½ cup chicken stock or broth
- sprigs of fresh rosemary, thyme, parsley, tarragon, or chives (or a mix)
- lemon wedges
- for the butter
- 4 tbsp unsalted butter, at room temperature
- 1 garlic clove, peeled and finely minced
- 2 tbsp chopped fresh herbs, such as rosemary, thyme, parsley, tarragon, or chives (or a mix)
- 2 tsp lemon zest
- 2 tsp freshly squeezed lemon juice
- ½ tsp coarse salt
- ½ tsp freshly ground black pepper

Directions:

1. Supply your smoker with wood pellets and follow the start-up procedure. Preheat the grill, with the lid closed, to 400° F.

2. In a small bowl, make the herb butter by combining the ingredients.

3. Place the chicken on a rimmed sheet pan and tuck the lemon rinds from the butter into the main cavity. Rub the outside of the chicken with the herb butter. (Reserve any remainder.) Tuck the wings behind the back and tie the legs together with butcher's twine. Place the onion wedges in a shallow roasting pan to help form a natural rack for the chicken. (Alternatively, place several large carrots, trimmed and peeled, on the bottom of the pan.) Place the chicken on the onion rack. Add the chicken stock and any remaining herbed butter and lemon juice.

4. Place the roasting pan on the grate, roast the chicken for 30 minutes, and then baste with the juices from the bottom of the pan. Baste every 15 minutes until the chicken is golden brown and the internal temperature reaches 165°F (74°C), about 45 minutes more.

5. Transfer the chicken to a cutting board and let rest for 10 minutes. Carve the chicken and place the slices on a platter with a deep well. Spoon some of the juices over the chicken. Scatter fresh herbs over the top. Serve with the lemon wedges.

COCKTAILS RECIPES

Smoked Jacobsen Salt Margarita

Servings: 2

Cooking Time: 1 Day

Ingredients:

- kosher sea salt
- 3 Cup Jacobsen Co. Honey
- 6 Ounce tequila
- 4 Ounce fresh squeezed lime juice
- 1/2 Cup Jacobsen Salt Co. Cherrywood Smoked Salt or smoked kosher salt
- 2 Ounce simple syrup
- 2 Teaspoon orange liqueur

Directions:

1. If making your own smoked salt, take kosher sea salt (however much you want to smoke) and spread it out on a tray.

2. Supply your smoker with wood pellets and follow the start-up procedure. Preheat the grill, with the lid closed, to 165° F.

3. Place tray of salt directly on the grill grate and smoke for about 24 hours, stirring the salt every 8 hours. Once it has smoked for 24 hours, take off grill and use in all your favorite dishes. Note: If you want to skip the long smoke session, use Jacobsen Salt Co. Cherrywood Smoked Salt. Grill: 165 ˚F

4. Simple Syrup: Put the honey and 1 cup water in a small saucepan. Cook over low heat, stirring, for about 20 min.

5. Fill a cocktail shaker with ice. Add tequila, lime juice, simple syrup and orange liqueur. Cover and shake until mixed and chilled, about 30 seconds.

6. Place smoked salt on a plate. Press the rim of a chilled rocks glass into the salt to rim the edge. Strain margarita into the glass. Enjoy!

Dublin Delight Cocktail

Servings: 2

Cooking Time: 20 Minutes

Ingredients:

- 2 orange, sliced
- 3 Fluid Ounce Teeling Whiskey
- 1 1/2 Fluid Ounce Smoked Simple Syrup
- 6 Dash aromatic bitters
- 6 Fluid Ounce Guinness beer
- 2 Amarena cherry, for garnish

Directions:

1. Supply your smoker with wood pellets and follow the start-up procedure. Preheat the grill, with the lid closed, to 450° F.

2. Place orange slices directly on the grill grate and cook 20 to 25 minutes. Remove from grill and let cool. Grill: 450 ˚F

3. In a mixing glass, add whiskey, Traeger Smoked Simple Syrup and bitters. Add ice and shake. Pour over a beer glass filled with ice and top off with cold Guinness.

4. Garnish with a grilled orange slice and Amarena cherry. Enjoy!

Grilled Rabbit Tail Cocktail

Servings: 2

Cooking Time: 25 Minutes

Ingredients:

- 1 1/2 Ounce lemon juice
- 4 Ounce Apple Brandy

- 1 Ounce orange juice
- 1 Ounce Smoked Simple Syrup

Directions:

1. Supply your smoker with wood pellets and follow the start-up procedure. Preheat the grill, with the lid closed, to 350° F.

2. Place lemon halves directly on the grill grate and cook for 20-25 minutes or until grill marks appear. Remove from grill and let cool. Once cool enough to handle, juice the lemons then chill and reserve the juice. Grill: 350 ℉

3. Using the proportions listed above and considering the size and consumption rate of your tailgate crew or party, mix all the above ingredients in a large thermos and top with a bit of ice.

4. Using 6-8 oz glasses or cups, guests can serve themselves from the thermos and garnish each drink with a grilled apple slice. Enjoy!

Grilled Peach Smash Cocktail

Servings: 2
Cooking Time: 10 Minutes

Ingredients:

- 2 peach, sliced and grilled
- 10 fresh mint leaves
- 1 1/2 Ounce Smoked Simple Syrup
- 4 Ounce bourbon
- 2 mint sprig, for garnish

Directions:

1. Supply your smoker with wood pellets and follow the start-up procedure. Preheat the grill, with the lid closed, to 375° F.

2. Cut the peach into 6 slices and brush with Traeger Smoked Simple Syrup. Place directly on the grill grate and cook 10 to 12 minutes or until peaches soften and get grill marks. Grill: 375 ℉

3. In a mixing glass, add 3 slices of grilled peaches, 5 mint leaves and Traeger Smoked Simple Syrup.

4. Muddle ingredients to release oils of the mint and juices from the grilled peaches. Add bourbon and crushed ice.

5. Shake and pour into a stemless wine glass. Top off with more crushed ice. Garnish with a grilled peach and mint sprig. Enjoy!

Grilled Blood Orange Mimosa

Servings: 4
Cooking Time: 15 Minutes

Ingredients:

- 3 blood orange, halved
- 2 Tablespoon granulated sugar
- 1 Bottle sparkling wine
- thyme sprigs, for garnish

Directions:

1. Supply your smoker with wood pellets and follow the start-up procedure. Preheat the grill, with the lid closed, to 375° F.

2. When the grill is hot, dip the cut side of the orange halves in sugar and place cut side down directly on the grill grate. Grill: 375 ℉

3. Grill the oranges for 10-15 minutes or until grill marks develop. Grill: 375 ℉

4. Remove from the grill and let cool at room temperature.

5. When cool enough to handle, juice the oranges and strain through a fine strainer removing any pulp.

6. Pour 5 oz of sparkling wine into each glass and top with 1 oz blood orange juice.

7. Garnish with a sprig of thyme. Enjoy!

Grilled Peach Mint Julep

Servings: 2

Cooking Time: 45 Minutes

Ingredients:

- 2 Whole peach
- 4 Ounce whiskey
- 2 Cup sugar
- 4 Tablespoon pink peppercorns
- 20 Whole fresh mint leaves, plus more for garnish
- 2 lime wedge, for garnish
- 4 Ounce bourbon

Directions:

1. For the Grilled Whiskey Peaches: cut peach into slices, then soak peach slices in whiskey in the refrigerator for 4 to 6 hours.
2. For the Pink Peppercorn Simple Syrup: In a shallow pan, combine sugar, 1 cup water and pink peppercorns.
3. Supply your smoker with wood pellets and follow the start-up procedure. Preheat the grill, with the lid closed, to 180° F.
4. Cook syrup down on the grill for 30 minutes, or until desired smoke flavor has been reached. Remove from the grill. Grill: 180 °F
5. Increase Traeger temperature to 350°F and preheat. Place the whiskey peach slices directly on the grill grate and cook 10 to 12 minutes or until peaches soften and get grill marks. Grill: 350 °F
6. To make the Julep: Muddle 1/2 ounce Pink Peppercorn Simple Syrup with 10 fresh mint leaves and 4 slices of grilled whiskey peaches.
7. Add crushed ice over the rim of the glass. Pour bourbon over the crushed ice and stir. Garnish with 1 large sprig of mint and fresh lime. Enjoy!

Smoked Pumpkin Spice Latte

Servings: 4

Cooking Time: 45 Minutes

Ingredients:

- 1 Small sugar pumpkin
- olive oil
- 1 Can sweetened condensed milk
- 1 Cup whole milk
- 2 Tablespoon Smoked Simple Syrup
- 1 Teaspoon pumpkin pie spice
- pinch of salt
- cinnamon
- whipped cream
- shaved nutmeg
- 8 Ounce smoked cold brew coffee

Directions:

1. Supply your smoker with wood pellets and follow the start-up procedure. Preheat the grill, with the lid closed, to 325° F.
2. Cut the sugar pumpkin in half, scoop out the seeds and discard. Place the pumpkin halves cut side up on a baking sheet and brush lightly with olive oil.
3. Place the sheet tray directly on the grill grate and cook 45 minutes or until the flesh is tender. Remove from heat and place on the counter to cool. Grill: 325 °F
4. When the pumpkin is cool enough to handle, scoop out the flesh and mash until smooth.
5. Place 3 Tbsp of the pumpkin puree in a separate bowl and reserve the remaining for another use.
6. Add the sweetened condensed milk, whole milk, Traeger Smoked Simple Syrup, pumpkin pie seasoning and salt to the pumpkin puree. Whisk to combine.
7. Pour the cold brew over ice, add desired amount of pumpkin spice creamer and top with whipped cream, cinnamon, and shaved nutmeg if desired. Enjoy!

Smoked Hibiscus Sparkler

Servings: 4
Cooking Time: 30 Minutes

Ingredients:

- 1/2 Cup sugar
- 2 Tablespoon dried hibiscus flowers
- 1 Bottle sparkling wine
- crystallized ginger, for garnish

Directions:

1. Supply your smoker with wood pellets and follow the start-up procedure. Preheat the grill, with the lid closed, to 180° F.
2. Place water in a shallow baking dish and place directly on the grill grate. Smoke the water for 30 minutes or until desired smoke flavor is achieved. Grill: 180 °F
3. Pour water into a small saucepan and add sugar and hibiscus flowers. Bring to a simmer over medium heat and cook until sugar is dissolved.
4. Strain out the hibiscus flowers and transfer your simple syrup to a small container and refrigerate until chilled.
5. Pour 1/2 ounce smoked hibiscus simple syrup in the bottom of a champagne glass and top with sparkling wine.
6. Drop in a few pieces of crystallized ginger to garnish. Enjoy!

Traeger Old Fashioned

Servings: 2
Cooking Time: 60 Minutes

Ingredients:

- 2 orange
- 2 Cup cherries
- 3 Ounce bourbon
- 1 Ounce Smoked Simple Syrup
- 8 Dash Bitters Lab Apricot Vanilla Bitters

Directions:

1. Supply your smoker with wood pellets and follow the start-up procedure. Preheat the grill, with the lid closed, to 180° F.
2. While Traeger preheats, slice whole orange into wheels.
3. Place cherries on a small sheet pan and place in the Traeger. Place orange slices directly on the grill grate.
4. Smoke cherries for 1 hour and oranges for 25 minutes, depending on taste, before removing from the grill. Let oranges and cherries cool. Grill: 180 °F
5. Pour bourbon into glass, followed by Traeger Smoked Simple Syrup and bitters. Add ice and stir for 45 seconds or until drink is well-diluted.
6. Strain contents into new glass over fresh ice. Skewer orange wheel and add cherry for garnish. Enjoy!

Smoked Grape Lime Rickey

Servings: 4
Cooking Time: 45 Minutes

Ingredients:

- 1/2 Pound red grapes
- 1/2 Cup plus 1 tablespoon sugar
- 1/2 Cup water
- 1 limes, sliced
- 2 limes, halved
- 1 Tablespoon sugar
- 1 L lemon lime soda

Directions:

1. Supply your smoker with wood pellets and follow the start-up procedure. Preheat the grill, with the lid closed, to 180° F.

2. Rinse grapes well and place in a shallow baking dish. Combine 1/2 cup sugar and water and stir until sugar dissolves. Pour over grapes.

3. Place the baking dish directly on the grill grate and smoke for 30 to 40 minutes until grapes are tender. Grill: 180 ˚F

4. Remove from the grill and pour entire contents of the baking dish in a blender. Puree on high until smooth then pass the mixture through a fine mesh strainer.

5. Increase Traeger temperature to 350˚F. Grill: 350 ˚F

6. Toss the lime slices and lime halves with 1 tablespoon sugar and place directly on the grill grate. Cook for 15 to 20 minutes or until grill marks develop. Remove from grill and set slices aside. When cool enough to handle, juice grilled lime halves. Grill: 350 ˚F

7. To build the drink, fill a pint glass with ice. Pour in 1-1/2 ounce grilled lime juice, 1-1/2 ounce smoked grape syrup and top off with soda. Garnish with grilled lime slice. Enjoy!

Smoked Salted Caramel White Russian

Servings: 4
Cooking Time: 20 Minutes

Ingredients:
- 16 Ounce half-and-half
- salted caramel sauce
- 6 Ounce vodka
- 6 Ounce Kahlúa

Directions:
1. Supply your smoker with wood pellets and follow the start-up procedure. Preheat the grill, with the lid closed, to 180° F.

2. Pour the half-and-half in a shallow baking dish and place directly on the grill grate. In another shallow baking dish, pour 2 to 3 cups of water and place on the grill next to the half-and-half.

3. Smoke both the half-and-half and water for 20 minutes. Remove from the grill and let cool. Grill: 180 ˚F

4. Place the half-and-half in the fridge until ready to use. Pour the smoked water into ice cube trays and transfer to the freezer until completely frozen.

5. Separate the smoked ice cubes into four glasses. Drizzle the salted caramel sauce around the inside of the glass.

6. Pour 1-1/2 ounce vodka and 1-1/2 ounce Kahlúa into each of the glasses and top with the smoked half-and-half. Enjoy!

Smoked Texas Ranch Water

Servings: 4
Cooking Time: 60 Minutes

Ingredients:
- 3 Whole limes
- 1 Tablespoon Blackened Saskatchewan Rub
- 12 Ounce blanco tequila
- 24 Ounce Topo Chico or other sparkling mineral water
- 8 Slices jalapeño, optional

Directions:
1. Supply your smoker with wood pellets and follow the start-up procedure. Preheat the grill, with the lid closed, to 225° F.

2. Cut two of the limes in half and sprinkle with Traeger Blackened Saskatchewan Rub. Place the four lime halves on the edge of the grill grate and

smoke for 1 hour. Remove from grill and set aside to cool. Grill: 225 ℉

3. Pour some of the rub onto a small plate. Cut the third lime into 1/4 wedges and use the lime to rub the rim of 4 cocktail glasses, turn the glasses upside down, and into the rub to salt the rim.

4. Place several ice cubes into your rimmed glasses and pour 3 ounces tequila, 6 ounces Topo Chico, squeeze the juice of one smoked lime (discard after squeezing), and add one fresh lime wedge to each. If using the jalapeño, add one or two slices to each glass (muddle if desired).

5. Stir to combine and enjoy!

Traeger Boulevardier Cocktail

Servings: 2
Cooking Time: 60 Minutes

Ingredients:

- 4 oranges
- 1/2 Cup honey
- 1500 mL rye whiskey
- 1 1/2 Ounce Campari
- 1 1/2 Ounce sweet vermouth
- 2 Tablespoon granulated sugar
- 3 Ounce grilled orange infused rye

Directions:

1. Supply your smoker with wood pellets and follow the start-up procedure. Preheat the grill, with the lid closed, to 350° F.

2. Slice 2 oranges in half and coat cut side with honey. Peel remaining orange and place peels on the grill. Cook 20 to 25 minutes. Grill: 350 ℉

3. Remove from grill and let cool. Place orange halves cut side down directly on the grill grate and cook 20 to 30 minutes or until dark grill marks appear. Remove orange halves and allow to cool. Grill: 350 ℉

4. Place orange halves into a bottle of rye whiskey and let steep for 10 to 12 hours. The longer they steep, the sweeter and more pronounced the orange flavor will be.

5. Add all ingredients into a mixing glass and stir until diluted. Strain into a fresh coupe glass and serve neat.

6. Garnish with grilled orange peel. Enjoy!

Smoked Barnburner Cocktail

Servings: 2
Cooking Time: 45 Minutes

Ingredients:

- 16 Ounce fresh raspberries
- 1/2 Cup Smoked Simple Syrup
- 1 1/2 Ounce smoked raspberry syrup
- 3 Ounce reposado tequila
- 1 Ounce lime juice
- 1 Ounce lemon juice
- 2 grilled lime wheel, for garnish

Directions:

1. Supply your smoker with wood pellets and follow the start-up procedure. Preheat the grill, with the lid closed, to 180° F.

2. For Smoked Raspberry Syrup: Place fresh raspberries on a grill mat and smoke for 30 minutes. After the raspberries have been smoked, reserve a few for garnish and place the remainder into a shallow sheet pan with Traeger Smoked Simple Syrup. Grill: 180 ℉

3. Place sheet pan on the grill grate and smoke for 45 minutes. Remove from grill and let cool. Strain through a fine mesh sieve discarding solids. Transfer the syrup to the refrigerator until ready to use. Makes about 1/2 cup of smoked raspberry syrup. Grill: 180 ℉

4. For cocktail: Add 3/4 ounce smoked raspberry syrup, tequila, lime juice and lemon juice with ice into a mixing glass. Shake and pour over clean ice. Garnish with smoked raspberries and a grilled lime wheel. Enjoy!

Smoky Scotch & Ginger Cocktail

Servings: 2

Cooking Time: 60 Minutes

Ingredients:

- 1 Ounce ginger syrup
- 1/2 Ounce brandied cherry juice
- 1/2 Ounce agave nectar
- 4 Ounce scotch
- 1 1/2 Ounce lemon juice
- 2 Slices grilled lemon, for garnish
- 2 cherry, for garnish

Directions:

1. Supply your smoker with wood pellets and follow the start-up procedure. Preheat the grill, with the lid closed, to 180° F.

2. For the smoked ginger cherry syrup: Place ginger syrup, cherry juice and agave nectar in a shallow dish and place the dish directly on the grill grate.

3. Smoke for 60 minutes, or until the mixture has picked up the smoke flavor. Remove from grill and allow to cool for 30 minutes. Grill: 180 °F

4. Place smoked ginger cherry syrup, scotch and lemon juice into a shaker tin and shake with ice. Strain into a glass over fresh ice and garnish with a grilled lemon wheel and cherry. Enjoy!

Smoked Cold Brew Coffee

Servings: 8

Cooking Time: 120 Minutes

Ingredients:

- 12 Ounce coarse ground coffee
- heavy cream or milk
- sugar

Directions:

1. Place half the coffee grounds in a plastic container and slowly pour 3-1/2 cups water over the top of the grounds. Add remaining grounds and pour another 3-1/2 cups water over the top in a circular motion.

2. Press the grounds down into the water using the back of a spoon. Cover and transfer to the refrigerator and let sit for 18 to 24 hours.

3. Remove from refrigerator and strain into a clean container through a fine mesh strainer or double layer of cheese cloth.

4. Supply your smoker with wood pellets and follow the start-up procedure. Preheat the grill, with the lid closed, to 180° F.

5. Pour cold brew into a shallow baking dish and place directly on the grill grate. Smoke for 1 to 2 hours depending on desired level of smoke. Grill: 180 °F

6. Remove from grill and place over an ice bath to cool. Drink as is over ice, with cream or sugar or use in your favorite coffee recipes. Enjoy!

Honey Glazed Grapefruit Shandy Cocktail

Servings: 2

Cooking Time: 20 Minutes

Ingredients:

- 4 grapefruits
- 4 Tablespoon honey
- granulated sugar
- 2 Ounce bourbon
- 1 Ounce Smoked Simple Syrup

- 4 Ounce honey glazed grilled grapefruit, juiced
- 2 Bottle Ballast Point Grapefruit Sculpin

Directions:

1. Supply your smoker with wood pellets and follow the start-up procedure. Preheat the grill, with the lid closed, to 375° F.
2. For the honey glazed grapefruit: Slice one grapefruit in half and coat with 2 tablespoons honey.
3. Take the other grapefruit and slice into wheels. Toss the wheels in granulated sugar until well coated.
4. Place the grapefruit halves and wheels directly on the grill grate, cut side down, and cook for 20 to 30 minutes. Remove from grill and set the wheels aside. Grill: 375 ℉
5. Squeeze the grapefruit halves into a measuring cup. It should yield about 2 oz juice.
6. Pour the grapefruit juice into a shaker and add bourbon and Traeger Smoked Simple Syrup then top with ice. Shake for 10-15 seconds.
7. Strain into glass, add ice and fill with beer. Garnish with the grilled grapefruit wheel. Enjoy!

Cran-apple Tequila Punch With Smoked Oranges

Servings: 2

Cooking Time: 15 Minutes

Ingredients:

- 6 Cup apple juice, chilled
- 6 Cup light cranberry cocktail
- 1 Cup cranberries, fresh or thawed
- 3 Large oranges, halved
- 1 Cup sugar, for rimming glasses
- 2 Tablespoon lemon juice
- 2 Cup reposado tequila
- 1 Cup orange-flavored liqueur, such as Grand Marnier or Cointreau
- 2 Bottle sparkling wine (such as prosecco) or sparkling water

Directions:

1. Combine 1 cup each of the apple and cranberry juices, then pour into ice cube trays. If the cube molds are big enough, place a few cranberries into each cube. Freeze for 6 hours to overnight.
2. Supply your smoker with wood pellets and follow the start-up procedure. Preheat the grill, with the lid closed, to 180° F.
3. Place the orange halves cut-side down on the grill and smoke for 15 minutes. Remove from the grill and juice oranges. Reserve smoked orange juice. Grill: 180 ℉
4. When ready to serve, place the sugar on a flat plate. Pour the lemon juice into a bowl that will fit the rim of each glass.
5. Carefully dip the rim of each glass in the lemon juice, then dip in the sugar to create a 1/8" sugar rim. Turn the glass right-side up and allow to dry for a few minutes before using.
6. Just before serving, mix the remaining apple juice, cranberry cocktail and smoked orange juice with the tequila, orange liqueur, and sparkling wine in a large bowl or pitcher. Taste, adding more of any ingredient to meet your preference.
7. When ready to serve, place a few ice cubes in each glass, then pour a cup of the punch over the top. Alternatively, place all of the ice cubes in the punch bowl and allow guests to help themselves. Enjoy!

Smoked Apple Cider

Servings: 2

Cooking Time: 30 Minutes

Ingredients:

- 32 Ounce apple cider
- 2 cinnamon sticks
- 4 whole cloves
- 3 star anise
- 2 Pieces orange peel
- 2 Pieces lemon peel

Directions:

1. Supply your smoker with wood pellets and follow the start-up procedure. Preheat the grill, with the lid closed, to 225° F.

2. Combine the cider, cinnamon stick, star anise, clove, lemon and orange peel in a shallow baking dish.

3. Place directly on the grill grate and smoke for 30 minutes. Remove from grill, strain and transfer to four mugs. Grill: 225 ˚F

4. Finish with a slice of apple and a cinnamon stick to serve. Enjoy!

Smoked Ice Mojito Slurpee

Servings: 2

Cooking Time: 30 Minutes

Ingredients:

- water
- 1 Cup white rum
- 1/2 Cup lime juice
- 1/4 Cup Smoked Simple Syrup
- 12 Whole fresh mint leaves
- 4 Sprig mint
- 4 Whole lime wedge, for garnish

Directions:

1. Supply your smoker with wood pellets and follow the start-up procedure. Preheat the grill, with the lid closed, to 180° F.

2. For optimal flavor, use Super Smoke if available. Grill: 180 ˚F

3. Remove water from grill and pour smoked water into ice cube trays. Place in freezer until frozen.

4. Add rum, lime juice, Traeger Smoked Simple Syrup, mint and smoked ice to a blender.

5. Blend until a slushy consistency and pour into glasses.

6. Garnish with a mint sprig and lime wedge. Enjoy!

Smoking Gun Cocktail

Servings: 2

Cooking Time: 45 Minutes

Ingredients:

- 2 Jar vermouth soaked cocktail onions
- 3 Ounce vodka
- 1 Ounce dry vermouth

Directions:

1. Supply your smoker with wood pellets and follow the start-up procedure. Preheat the grill, with the lid closed, to 180° F.

2. To make the smoked onion vermouth: Pour jar of vermouth soaked cocktail onions onto a shallow sheet pan. Smoke for 45 minutes. Remove from grill and set aside to chill. Grill: 180 ˚F

3. To make the cocktail: Add vodka, 1 teaspoon liquid from the smoked onions and dry vermouth to a mixing glass. Shake and strain into a chilled martini glass.

4. Garnish with smoked cocktail onions on a skewer. Enjoy!

Grilled Frozen Strawberry Lemonade

Servings: 4
Cooking Time: 15 Minutes

Ingredients:

- 1 Pound fresh strawberries
- 1/2 Cup turbinado sugar
- 8 lemon, halved
- 1/4 Cup Cointreau
- 1/4 Cup simple syrup
- 2 Cup ice
- 1 Cup Titos Vodka

Directions:

1. Supply your smoker with wood pellets and follow the start-up procedure. Preheat the grill, with the lid closed, to High heat.

2. Dip the lemon halves in turbinado sugar and place directly on the grill grate. Toss the strawberries with remaining sugar and place next to the lemons.

3. Cook until grill marks develop on both, about 15 min for lemons and 10 min for strawberries.

4. Remove from heat and let cool.

5. Juice grilled lemons straining out any seeds or pulp. Pour into a blender pitcher.

6. Remove stems from grilled strawberries and place in blender pitcher with lemon juice. Add simple syrup, vodka, cointreau, and 2 cups of ice.

7. Puree until smooth and transfer to 4-6 glasses. Garnish with grilled strawberries and grilled lemon slices if desired. Enjoy!

Bacon Old-fashioned Cocktail

Servings: 2
Cooking Time: 20 Minutes

Ingredients:

- 16 Slices bacon
- 1/2 Cup warm water (110°F to 115°F)
- 1500 mL bourbon
- 1/2 Fluid Ounce maple syrup
- 4 Dash Angostura bitters
- 2 fresh orange peel

Directions:

1. Smoke bacon prior to making Old Fashioned using this recipe for Applewood Smoked Bacon.

2. To Make Bacon: Supply your smoker with wood pellets and follow the start-up procedure. Preheat the grill, with the lid closed, to 325° F.

3. Place bacon in a single layer on a cooling rack that fits inside a baking sheet pan. Cook in Traeger for 15-20 minutes or until bacon is browned and crispy. Reserve bacon for later. Let the fat cool slightly; you'll use the fat to infuse the bourbon. Grill: 325 °F

4. Combine 1/4 cup of warm (not hot) liquid bacon fat with the entire contents of a 750ml bottle of bourbon in a glass or heavy plastic container.

5. Use a fork to stir well. Let it sit on the counter for a few hours, stirring every so often.

6. After about four hours, put bourbon fat mixture into the freezer. After about an hour, the fat will congeal and you can simply scoop it out with a spoon. You can fine-strain the mixture through a sieve to remove all fat if desired.

7. Combine ingredients with ice and stir until cold. Strain over fresh ice in an Old Fashioned glass and garnish with reserved bacon and orange peel. Enjoy!

Smoked Pomegranate Lemonade Cocktail

Servings: 2

Cooking Time: 45 Minutes

Ingredients:

- 32 Ounce POM Juice
- 2 Cup pomegranate seeds
- 3 Ounce vodka
- 8 Ounce lemonade
- lemon wheel, for garnish
- fresh mint, for garnish

Directions:

1. Supply your smoker with wood pellets and follow the start-up procedure. Preheat the grill, with the lid closed, to 225° F.

2. For the Smoked Pomegranate Ice Cubes: Pour one small container of POM juice and 1 cup of pomegranate seeds into a shallow sheet pan. Smoke on the Traeger for 45 minutes. Pull off grill and let sit until cooled. Grill: 180 °F

3. Pour smoked POM juice into ice molds of your choice and put into freezer.

4. When ready to serve, place the frozen pomegranate cubes into a mason jar. Pour vodka and lemonade over the ice cubes.

5. Garnish with a lemon wheel and fresh mint. Enjoy!

Ryes And Shine Cocktail

Servings: 2

Cooking Time: 30 Minutes

Ingredients:

- 2 lemon, cut into wheels for garnish
- 6 Tablespoon granulated sugar
- 2 Ounce rye
- 1 Ounce bourbon
- 3 Ounce lemon juice
- 1 Ounce Smoked Simple Syrup
- 6 Dash Fernet-Branca

Directions:

1. Supply your smoker with wood pellets and follow the start-up procedure. Preheat the grill, with the lid closed, to 325° F.

2. Toss lemon wheels with granulated sugar to coat on both sides. Place wheels directly on the grill grate and cook for 15 minutes on each side or until grill marks form. Grill: 325 °F

3. Add rye, bourbon, lemon juice, Traeger Smoked Simple Syrup and Fernet-Branca to a shaker and shake until slightly diluted (about 10 to 15 seconds).

4. Pour into a fresh glass, serve neat and garnish with a grilled lemon wheel. Enjoy!

Smoked Irish Coffee

Servings: 2

Cooking Time: 15 Minutes

Ingredients:

- 10 Ounce hot coffee
- 1/2 Cup heavy cream
- 1 Tablespoon sugar
- 2 Ounce Irish whiskey
- freshly grated nutmeg, for garnish (optional)

Directions:

1. Supply your smoker with wood pellets and follow the start-up procedure. Preheat the grill, with the lid closed, to 180° F.

2. Place the coffee and cream in separate shallow baking dishes and place both directly on the grill grate. Smoke for 10 to 15 minutes until the liquids pick up a slight smoke flavor. Grill: 180 °F

3. Remove from the grill and cool the cream. When the cream is cool, add sugar and whip in a stand mixer or by hand to soft peaks.

4. Pour the hot coffee into two mugs then add 2 ounces of whiskey to each.

5. Top with smoked whipped cream and finish with freshly grated nutmeg, if desired. Enjoy!

Delicious Deviled Crab Appetizer 100
Delicious Pellet Grill Cornbread 31
Delicious Pulled Pork Poutine 57
Delicious Smoked Turketta 111
Deviled Eggs With Smoked Paprika 96
Dijon-smoked Halibut 25
Dublin Delight Cocktail 118

E
Easy Bbq Chicken Wings 107
Easy Breakfast Cheeseburger 85

F
First-timer's Pulled Pork 55
Flavour Fire Spiced Shrimp 27
Flavour Memphis Bbq Beef Brisket 81
Flavour Smoked Chuck Roast 80
Florentine Shrimp Al Cartoccio 18
Focaccia 36

G
Garlic Blackened Catfish 15
Garlic Cheese Bacon Burger 88
Green Bean Casserole 69
Green Bean Casserole Circa 1955 42
Green Chile Chicken Enchiladas 108
Grilled Albacore Tuna With Potato-tomato
Casserole 26
Grilled Artichoke Cheese Salmon 19
Grilled Asparagus And Spinach Salad 61
Grilled Beer Cheese Dip 30
Grilled Blood Orange Mimosa 119
Grilled Cheesy Chicken 113
Grilled Chili-lime Corn 72
Grilled Fingerling Potato Salad 67
Grilled Frozen Strawberry Lemonade 127
Grilled Garlic Shrimp With Cajun Dip 16
Grilled Garlic Tomahawk Steak 79

Grilled Greek Chicken With Garlic & Lemon
105
Grilled Guacamole 95
Grilled Lemon Pepper Pork Tenderloin 50
Grilled Lemon Salmon 27
Grilled Peach Mint Julep 120
Grilled Peach Smash Cocktail 119
Grilled Prosciutto Wrapped Asparagus 47
Grilled Rabbit Tail Cocktail 118
Grilled Raspberry Chipotle Pork Ribs 59
Grilled Ratatouille Salad 63
Grilled Rib Eyes With Hasselback Sweet
Potatoes 81
Grilled Rosemary Rack Of Lamb 82
Grilled Whole Steelhead Fillet 17

H
Hawaiian Pineapple Pork Butt 47
Hawaiian Pulled Pork 54
Honey Glazed Grapefruit Shandy Cocktail 124
Hot-smoked Salmon 23

I
Irish Pasties 82
Irish Soda Bread 33
Italian Meatballs 86

J
Jalapeño- & Cheese-stuffed Chicken 115
Jalapeño Beef Jerky 87
Jalapeño Poppers With Chipotle Sour Cream 101
Jamaican Jerk Pork Chops 52

K
Kimi's Simple Grilled Fresh Fish 26

L
Lemon & Herb Chicken 117
Lemon Lobster Rolls 21
Lobster Tail 20

Smoked Jalapeño Poppers 70
Smoked Mashed Potatoes 69
Smoked Mushrooms 62
Smoked Pheasant 83
Smoked Pickled Green Beans 71
Smoked Pomegranate Lemonade Cocktail 128
Smoked Pumpkin Spice Latte 120
Smoked Salted Caramel White Russian 122
Smoked Seed Pastrami 84
Smoked Sweet Beer Bread 37
Smoked Teriyaki Jerky 85
Smoked Texas Ranch Water 122
Smoked Turkey Sandwich 101
Smoked Whole Chicken 110
Smoking Gun Cocktail 126
Smoky Scotch & Ginger Cocktail 124
Spiced Bbq Turkey 113
Spiced Coffee-rubbed Ribs 51
Sriracha & Maple Cashews 101
Strawberry Basil Daiquiri 44
Sweet And Spicy Baked Pork Beans 43
Sweet Cheese Muffins 41

T
Tarte Tatin 41

Tater Tot Bake 61
Teriyaki Smoked Honey Tilapia 23
Texas Smoked Brisket 86
Traeger Bacon-wrapped Filet Mignon 90
Traeger Bbq Brisket 79
Traeger Boulevardier Cocktail 123
Traeger Cajun Broil 50
Traeger Grilled Whole Corn 67
Traeger Old Fashioned 121
Traeger Roasted Easter Ham 49
Traeger Smoked Coleslaw 63
Triple Threat Pork Fattywith Stuffed Jalapeños 46

V
Vanilla Chocolate Bacon Cupcakes 31
Vanilla Chocolate Chip Cookies 32

W
Whole Roasted Cauliflower With Garlic Parmesan Butter 64
Wild West Wings 104

Y
Yucatán-spiced Chicken Thighs 106